A Quorum of
another look at Wi

Patricia Rowland

Willa Muir came to me by accident. I had intended to write not about her, but about her husband, Edwin Muir, yet somewhere in my first year of research she appeared – "strong-willed, firm-lipped, and decisive", to use the words of Robert Bruce Lockhart – and stood, almost hands on hips, staring me in the face. Until then she'd been the quintessential silent wife.

This woman, who Lockhart went on to describe with admirable restraint as "the more aggressive of the two", a Madame Defarge *sans* knitting needles, was born Wilhelmina Johnstone Anderson at Montrose, in 1890 and lived there until she left in 1907 for St Andrews University. In *Belonging*, her autobiography, she recalls how she never felt at home in Montrose, where, she says, at the age of three she stood in Bridge Street, "fingering my pinafore, dumb with embarrassment, while four or five older girls squealed in delighted mockery of what I had been saying and urged me to say it again." She soon learned "broad Scots", but to the end of her life she denied any affinity with her childhood home, instead she claimed her parents' Scots-Nordic heritage as her own. She was a Shetlander, she would say, and that was that.

Looking from the outside in, the observant three-year-old would reach the end of her life still wondering who she was and where she fitted in. In an unpublished story about a young bursary student living on the east coast of Scotland, Willa opens with the narrator proclaiming that "Elizabeth lived in a state of latent indignation." Sixty years have passed since the indignant Elizabeth was created and over twenty years since the author's death, yet the autobiographical discontent still resounds with astonishing clarity. When she wrote *Belonging* Willa was over seventy, and apparently had made her peace with the young Elizabeth still in the making in this unpublished fragment – the feisty young student who pondered why girls were treated so unfairly and grumbled when her younger brother was allowed to stay out later than she was. By then she was no longer a character romanticised by fiction but an aging, crippled widow, living alone in a basement flat, inching her way through her days remembering a life which no longer existed. Comparing the woman in the autobiography and unpublished stories to the one in the diaries and letters however, I sense that her peace was little more than a series of temporary truces, moments of peaceful coexistence between her mature mind and the disquiet she'd felt from the start.

Judith Viorst, in her book *Necessary Losses*, states that many students of ageing believe the core of one's personality remains constant throughout life. "We are, in old age, the person we've always been, except maybe more so," she says. Then, tempering what to some might seem cynicism, she adds that it's not that people *can't* change but that many simply *don't*. If we remain what we are, "only more so", to the very end, then the responses to life Willa had as a young woman would be similar to those she had while living out her last years in Cambridge, London and Dunoon.

Physically Willa changed over the years: the student A S Neill remembered as capable of out-walking her companions, who in the Elizabeth fragment "took to her heels down the lane" feeling "as if she could run forever", ended her life crippled by arthritis, barely able to care for her simplest needs. "It is bad", she wrote of her physical condition to Ernest and Jeanette Marwick (21 July 1959). "I have to hirple from room to room… We [she and her son Gavin] have two anthracite stoves and it's as much as I can manage to put on a shovelful now and then and shut them up again. I have to sit down and recover after that!" To find the telling details, one must look beyond the physical. This hirpling from room to room was what she called an "accidental"; what really mattered was something deeper, something her own surface humour could scarcely hide. In 1947, for Edwin's sixtieth birthday, she wrote:

> I hope that old age makes me merely comic,
> a funny, fat old woman with false teeth,
> that click or treacherously clack together,
> and bosom bursting from a straining sheath,
> vast hips and creaking knees and hobbling feet
> enveloped in a merciful skirt and cloak,
> a shameless old grey head, and mounted on it
> some foolish trifle of a hat or bonnet
> or even – God be good to us – a toque!
>
> I was not born to be a comic figure,
> but life has changed me into one at last.
> I hope, my love, you will not find me tedious
> although my double chins are doubling fast,
> and till I die find merriment in me;
> but when I'm dead among the elementals
> I hope you will forget the accidentals
> remembering rather what I meant to be.

Charles University in Prague had bestowed an honorary doctorate on Edwin and in the midst of all the accolades and attendant celebrations, Willa was asking him to remember the person beside him – to look beyond her prematurely aging body and see the person she'd meant to be. She wasn't a buffoon but someone whose dreams he'd shared when they fell in love years earlier in Glasgow. Physical changes were only "accidentals", she reminds him, then asking that he remember *not* what she'd become but what she'd "meant to be," her comparison slips. She moves from the accidental *exterior* of the present-day Willa to the not-yet-realised *interior* of the person she'd once been. If she'd wanted to hide her insecurities, she failed, for it's in the interior – the region where mind and soul mingle to imagine what might be – that the core is found.

The early Elizabeth fragment gives a clue to Willa's thoughts when she'd asked Edwin to remember what she'd "meant to be." The narrator says that "to do things spontaneously, even capriciously, but always brilliantly was Elizabeth's recognised part in the life of the class." They were qualities not universally appreciated, however, and the story makes it clear that her family expected something else entirely. They wanted mediocrity – a daughter who responded to her preordained role without questioning it. She had to tutor her younger brother, "who couldn't do his lessons without her help", the narrator says, and wipe the supper dishes without having to be asked. Then, as if this weren't enough, she had to be in by ten when her brother could stay out past eleven. Being a docile female was *not* what she wanted. While she detested the male dominance she saw all around her, championing the feminist cause wasn't her primary concern. Even if it had been, Willa's opinions were too inconsistent to be taken seriously. In another unpublished work, *Mrs. Muttoe and the Top Storey*, the main protagonist is a translator of books whose work is equal to her husband's – "The Muttoes must be like twins, doing everything together," says the newly hired maid as she watches them retire into separate offices each morning – yet after pages of didactics on the relationship between mind and feeling, "the top storey" versus "the centre," the manuscript ends with the not-so-strong female clasping her husband's hand for support. "Dick's hand groped towards her and she caught it and clung to it." In *The Bridge*, another unpublished story, the wife attempts to leave her husband, who doesn't properly understand her, then changes her mind, returns, rescues him from sleepwalking dangerously close to a construction scaffolding, and ends up "crumpled and sobbing at his feet."

If fighting the feminist cause wasn't Willa's calling in life, neither was righting the inequality of the class system, which, the narrator of the Elizabeth fragment says, "made the prestige denied her by her humble birth difficult to attain." She goes on to say, "The Clarks were a step above her in the social scale", distinctions which "fretted" her; then analysing the social factors which resulted in Elizabeth not being invited to a party, she adds, "Where work or mischief was the only consideration Elizabeth led the class by natural right. But in the Latin class where there was a certain intimacy between master and pupils, her social inferiority appeared." Willa had as much regard for the inequalities of the British class system as for male chauvinism and later depicted the foibles of her fellow Scots in *Imagined Corners*, the social snobbism of an entire nation in *Mrs Grundy in Scotland*, and her husband's position in the British Council in *The Usurpers,* all of them works questioning or making light of a person's decreed place in society. Again, however, none of this appears to have been enough to still the restlessness within her. When, late in life, she gave a lecture at St Andrews, and J B Salmond had shown "great apparent friendliness and warmth" publicly, afterwards ignoring her completely, the ache was deeper. She wrote in her journal, "I had a blankness, a failure of something that I had expected to find." Being treated unfairly as a female and having to endure the inequality of the

4

social position given her at birth were nothing compared to being obliterated as the person she knew herself to be.

In the Elizabeth fragment Willa, through her alter-ego, is seen sitting in class writing her name across the top of her desk while awaiting her exam results. She

> could not look up... The swots had beaten her. That conceited ass John Mackay was first. Even Sandy Moir had beaten her. If it had been Mathematics, which depended almost entirely on mugging up formulae, or if it had been French, which nobody took seriously, or even Latin or Greek, where one could pardonably make howlers, she would not have felt so disgraced. But English! Well, it was not exactly English; it was History, and she could not be bothered with dates and facts. Whatever it was, her confidence in her own ingenuity and artifice was terribly shaken. Night after night she had run about with Janet, scamping her work. In Latin and Greek her persistent neglect of preparation had only sharpened her flair for unseen translation, but her Latin proses were always spoilt by careless mistakes in grammar. Her English essays were her chief pride: what if they too were showy and not solid?

When the instructor walks over to her desk and jerks her pencil out of her hand, Elizabeth is mortified but briefly thinks he's spiteful because he's seen his caricature scribbled on her desk. She soon realises that even that consolation wasn't enough, not when faced with the real question: "Was she incapable of real brilliance?"

This intelligent, often critical woman, who Janet Adam Smith said "would play second fiddle to no man", translated dozens of novels and plays, some of them jointly with her husband, wrote six books – two of fiction and four non-fiction (one unpublished) – and wrote an assortment of radio scripts, short stories, diaries and letters; yet the person who had been class representative, founded the Literary and Debating Society, and led her classmates "by natural right", doubted her abilities from the start – doubts she never fully overcame. In a journal entry dated 20 August 1953, six years after writing the Prague poem, Willa rips through layers of doubt and denial and comes as close to the truth as she ever would. Edwin was in the process of revising his autobiography, *The Story and the Fable*, and had asked her advice on how to handle the Gerda incident at Hellerau thirty years earlier*. They discussed it while walking in the gardens of Newbattle Abbey College – with Willa predicting that he would ignore that segment of their lives when he came to write it – and eventually turned to other long-buried issues:

> Why I am to be described as a mess.
> Yesterday afternoon, walking the garden with Edwin, we discussed the part of our life, first visit to Italy, which he is writing about now in his autobiography. I suggested that it was because he was going to miss out so much: for instance, I was sure he would leave out the Gerda episode.

---

*Edwin had been given a letter by Gerda Krupp, a Hallerau student and translator of his poems, where she confessed her love for him. Willa tells her version of the "incident" in *Belonging*; there is no mention of it in *The Story and the Fable* or *An Autobiography*.

Yes, indeed he would, he said.

We began talking it over. I found I still could call up vividly the emotions of that terrible time, especially when we got to Riva, and one day in Tremosine when Edwin thought the walls were going to fall in on him every time we climbed at all high. The dull misery behind these brilliant blue days in the white powdery dust, I felt it all again. And I reminded Edwin how it had poisoned my pious pilgrimage to Catullus's *Sirmione.*

"What *did* she do to you?" I asked. "She must have felt your emotional state was vulnerable, and launched a shaft of power into it."

"Something like that," he said.

"Would it have been better for you to go back to her?" I asked.

"Don't be silly", he said. But I remembered the agony with which I walked on the wet beach of Garda, walking through the waves without even noticing that my shoes were soaking, as I wrestled with my misery, in the half-moonlight, alone, and then went back to tell Edwin that if he wanted to leave me in Italy and go back to Gerda, he should do it.

"That was what cured me", said Edwin. I did not remind him or myself that we had only one joint passport and very little money, and that I did not know what would become of me if he did go; although at the time I was very aware of it.

Edwin at that time felt, I think, that he had to answer any demand made on his affections by other people. I am sure he had never thought of being in love with Gerda, but when she took his arm on the way to the station and told him that she loved him passionately he felt he had to return her love. In the train he had a vile headache. In Riva he was sullen, sleepless and miserable; when he finally told me what had happened and said he felt he must go back to Hellerau, to Gerda, I was distraught.

Then he felt we *had* to go to Forte dei Marmi to the cottage with John Holms and Dorothy Jennings, because John had written imploring him to come, and saying he and Dorothy could not afford to live in the cottage alone, unless someone shared the expense.

I shrank from doing so. John Holms exasperated me, with his public-school attitudes, especially to women. (At any rate, to me.) He and [Hugh] Kingsmill treated women as powers to be propitiated at times, to be despised at other times, and never as rational partners in an intelligent life. So they, or each of them, talked exclusively to Edwin, simply leaving me out, whenever the conversation came as usual to literature, or literary men. I should have laughed at them, but I felt resentful, being young and inexperienced. I did react. So I shrank from going to join Holms, but because Edwin felt we *had* to, we went.

We reminded each other about Holms's greedy selfishness at the meals in the garden. How he came between me and Italy! Looking at a new scene, I would be sickened by Holms's drawl: 'Pure Botticelli, don't you think?' Edwin said he never felt in touch with Italy during these six months. I said, that was probably because of Holms.

To me it seemed we were in touch sufficiently with the purely local life, The girls gabbling their "Maggio" in the village of an evening. The warm tenor voices in the lanes, singing at two in the morning. The peasants thrusting sardines and carrots and tomatoes through the window above my bed at five in the morning. The little girl with the loud voice yelling the same vulgar song daily as she fetched water from the well. Teresa, our beautiful maid. Micino, the wild cat and her wilder kitten in the hedge. The *guardiana*, in especial, carrying a trunk on her head all the two miles from the village, knitting as she went and slopping in heelless mules all the time, rope-soled sandals with only blue hemp toe-covers.

Then there were our hours in the warm sea, where I managed to teach Edwin to swim. The walking tour on the Carrara mountains, and the farm family who sheltered us from the rain. The marble quarries – the flowered rose marble/The bank comedy over the "exchange". Shopping in Viareggio. The trip to Lerici.

The local *vino nero*.

Well, churning up these past events brought up in me a surprising rush of angry feeling that I had thought was long past and done with. The misery, the resentment, the irritations were all present again. I began to understand this revivification when I went on to talk about the evil effect on me of John Holms's persistent belittlement of me – or what I felt as his belittlement – and felt that I had a great lack of underlying confidence except in matters where I had proved my competence. For instance having done so much translation with success at the University, I was confident that I could translate, and so began doing it without *arriére-pensée* at Sonntagberg. But I had no general self-confidence – in writing literature, at least – and was easily cast down and shaken. For instance, when Edwin deplored my attempt in Dresden to write a Noah's Ark play in contemporary language, I gave it up. (Someone else did it, years after, successfully.) And when Edwin ignored the Usurpers – !! Then I unpacked all the unhappiness that had made my life bitter after finishing that novel – then I perceived well enough that the earlier bitter feelings had been only an excuse for realising the later. I really did let them all out. Edwin said, once, when we came back to the house: I don't think we should say any more about it; but I felt that these things *should* be talked out, to prevent their festering inside. Edwin finally said: "I'm afraid, you know, that I haven't got much sense". – Which is true of both of us.

And then I told him that even the translations I had done were no longer my own territory, for everyone assumes that Edwin did them. He is referred to as "THE" translator. By this time he may even believe that he was. He has let my reputation sink, by default; so now I fear that if the Feuchtwanger publishers are told that *I* am prepared to do his beastly novel, they will refuse unless Edwin engages to do it, or to put his name to it.

And the fact remains; I am a better translator than he is. The whole current of patriarchal society is set against this fact, however, and sweeps it into oblivion, simply because I did not insist on shouting aloud: "Most of this translation, especially Kafka, has been done by ME. Edwin only helped." And every time Edwin was referred to as THE translator, I was too proud to say anything; and Edwin himself felt it would be undignified to speak up, I suppose. So that now, especially since my breakdown in the middle of the war, I am left without a shred of literary reputation. And I am ashamed of the fact that I feel it as a grievance. It shouldn't bother me, Reputation is a passing value, after all. Yet it is now that I feel it, now when I am trying to build up my life again and overcome my disabilities: my dicky backbone, for instance, Because I seem to have nothing to build on, except that I am Edwin's wife and he still loves me. That is much. It is almost all, in a sense, that I could need. It is more than I deserve. And I know, too, how destructive ambition is, and how it deforms what one might create. And yet, and yet, I want to be acknowledged. That is why I say: I am a mess.

The schoolgirl who doubted her brilliance, the writer who created female protagonists at once independent and clinging, the woman who bristled at the social snobbism of her neighbours and rankled at the pettiness of the Lowland Scots were all present. A quorum of Willas. The antagonism that had been latent in the beginning sprang to life as if it were a beast uncaged and while she couldn't rid herself of all that she felt, by facing what lay at the core of her pain, she could lessen it at least for the moment. The Elizabeth who in the early fragment "passionately desired to shine" and felt that "intellectual distinction provided the only means of securing that prestige denied her by her humble birth" was able to say that no matter how much her mind told her otherwise – that one's reputation was of passing value, that having Edwin's love should be enough, that ambition was destructive – she still wanted to be acknowledged.

Two years before the August 1953 entry, Willa had worried about Edwin's reputation and hers after their deaths. "[His] poems will live," she wrote in her journal on January 15, 1951, "but of himself only a legend. Of me, only a very distorted legend... I doubt we should recognise ourselves in other people's memories of us." She knew the process of history – knew where images begin and how they grow and change and become in the end something else altogether. In her notes for *Belonging* she wrote that "no human being [could] ever see another human being straight, much less see himself straight," yet her mortal self wanted to be known just the same. Paradoxically, beyond that part of her that feared how she would be remembered, existed a wisdom which enabled her to write that "an absolute truth is a stopping-place, while life has no stopping-places since it is a continuing process that moves on as one looks at it."

Jean Strouse, writing on the art of biography in *Extraordinary Lives*, says that while the twentieth century may eventually be characterised by its "sense of fragmentation...its loss of consensus about what an 'exemplary' life might be, [we] still long for models of wholeness...for evidence that individual lives and choices matter." She then reminds us that "modern biography tells not *how to live*, but how other people, in all their interesting, quirky, original variety, have lived." And so it is with Willa. By examining her life – comparing her published work with her unpublished diaries and letters, speaking with those who knew her, analysing Edwin's perceptions as opposed to hers, seeking out the unexpected, telling detail, we see not how to live, but how *she* lived – and how she and her choices mattered. Yet even if we succeed in disentangling the various and often invisible threads of her life, or by insistent prodding, or sheer luck, put to rest some of the doubts she carried with her to the end, we will not have the last word. *That* was hers. Life *is* a continuing process and moves on even as I write.

Patricia Rowland Mudge

'Elizabeth' fragment

Willa Muir

Elizabeth lived in a state of latent indignation. Her younger brother George already over topped her by half a head, and her mother's ideal of womanhood was purely domestic. It was as much from an uneasy feeling that she was expected to dry the dishes as from an interest in Matty's conversation that she lingered near the sink where Matty was scrubbing the herring plates with soda. "Ay," said Matty, "he's gaen tae marry her, but it's forcework. Ye ken what I mean? An' there's nae guid ever comes o' tha-at."

"Why not?" demanded Elizabeth.

"Maist men juist likes ye till they've had what they wanted, an' then they wad fling ye awa' like an auld clout, marriage or nae marriage." Matty wrung out the dishcloth and took up the drying-towel. Her eye travelled to the drawer where the other dishtowels lay.

"I'm going out with Janet Clark", said Elizabeth promptly, pretending that she did not know what Matty was going to say.

"That's a wild lassie."

"She's nothing of the kind!" Elizabeth pulled her hat off the lobby peg. Matty should mind her own business. As she opened the stair door her mother's voice cried from the big bedroom: "Lizzie, where are you going?"

"Out", said Elizabeth banging the door and clattering downstairs. Her mother called out of the stair window, and in spite of herself Elizabeth heard plainly the words "ten o'clock!" Her temper rose as she ran past the washing-house. George could stay out till eleven, and only be asked where he had been. And he was fourteen months younger than she was, and couldn't do his lessons without her help. Why should girls be treated so unfairly?

But as she came out of the close into the High Street of Rossie the walls within which she brooded fell away. The High Street was wide, half-cobbled and half-smooth because it had once been two streets, and opposite Elizabeth's house it was widened still further by a gap among the gable-ends leading down to the estuary. The air on the east coast of Scotland sharpens landscapes to a hard brilliance, and Elizabeth, leaning against the mouth of the close, could see the far ridges of the Rossie hills over the water. Behind them the western sky was full of colour, and as she watched scarlet-and-gold changing slowly to purple-and-rose she struggled again to finish her poem on the sunset. "Just above the hills a tender space of quiet green… A tender space of quiet green looks out."

As she meditated she looked absently down the street towards the Clarks' house. The Clarks were a step above her in the social scale. Mr Clark sat in an office above the shop, and merely supervised his painters and decorators, while Elizabeth's mother stood all day behind the counter of her drapery emporium. Janet had been at the Academy since she was six, while Elizabeth had only entered it two years ago as a Town Bursar. These distinctions fretted Elizabeth, but she could not bring herself to ignore them and go unasked to the Clarks' door. Besides, the door might be opened by Chalmers Clark.

She had never spoken to Chalmers Clark. He sat at the end of the Clarks' pew just across the aisle in church, and when they stood up to sing the hymns he was quite near her. Elizabeth, as she sang in what she hoped was an enchanting voice, "Faint not nor fear/ His arm is near;/ He changeth not and thou art dear", felt her heart swell.

Yesterday she had conspired with Janet to send him a postcard on which were printed in a disguised script insulting quotations about tall men, all that Elizabeth could remember. Such as "Wert thou so tall to reach the Pole/ Or grasp the ocean in thy span,/ Thou must be measured by thy soul;/ The mind's the measure of the man." On this very evening three show tickets from the drapery emporium were secreted in her pocket. One of hem was to be pinned on Chalmers's coat-tail, so that he would be advertised to the world as "Only 1/11d a yard."

By the sudden racing of her heart she knew that a tall figure coming down the street was he. If only Janet had been there! She was afraid of blushing as he passed, and decided to look fixedly at the Central Hotel across the street. Her eyes felt strained: it was just like having one's photograph taken.

The thin long-legged boy strode down the pavement, one hand in his trouser pocket, an aloof expression on his white face. Elizabeth, staring at the Central Hotel, saw him as one sees a flash of lightning at the back of one's head. Perhaps he thought of her too. But Elizabeth disbelieved the idea, although she allowed herself to imagine it. Suppose that Rossie was besieged by a hostile army, and the food in the town ran short. The Town Council would give an order that all the inhabitants were to kill themselves rather than surrender. Chalmers Clark, pale and determined, would come and say, Elizabeth, we must die tomorrow. Let us be married today.

A vigorous punch shivered her dream and raised her sweetly bent head. "Hullo Elizabeth!" It was Janet Clark. They walked up the High Street looking for mischief. The shiny apples on Bond the grocer's apple-barrel attracted Elizabeth: she knew that Bond spat on them daily and polished them on the seat of his trousers. She stuck "Chic, 2/6 a pair" on the edge of the barrel, while Janet inserted the other ticket in a string of onions. Then, giggling, they darted down one of the long narrow lanes which run between the walled gardens at the back of the High Street houses. In these damp earthy lanes there is a fine security: the high brick walls on either side are crowned with bottle-glass and clumps of dark ivy, and things can be said there which appear furtive when one comes back into the High Street through another close.

Janet brought out of her pocket a sheet of typewritten paper and unfolded it. A girl in her father's office who was in touch with the circulating literature of the town lent her one or two every week.

"This one's about Gillespie."

Gillespie was the big mill-owner of Rossie. His jute mills hummed over one quarter of the links, and employed nearly all the women in the town. Every morning at six the town bell rang for five minutes, and the women and girls streamed through the big gates while the whistle shrieked, the elder women with shawls over their working gowns and men's caps on their heads, the younger with rows of Hinde's curlers and ordinary coats and skirts. Flecked with tow, bawling to each other in factory-trained voices, they came out at nine o'clock for an hour, filling the kirkyard walk down which Elizabeth went to school. She hated meeting them.

She read the manuscript. It was a folk-ballad, a scandalous history of how Gillespie took his secretary out driving in his carriage, and then overcame her faint scruples in a well-known local wood. Gillespie's prowess was celebrated in racy Scots.

> His bonny lass o' dossie broon
> Did jink and diddle;
> Was ever seen in a' the toon
> Sic bow, sic fiddle?

Elizabeth felt deliciously wicked; it was just like sniffing the big brandy bottle in the medicine cupboard.

"I've got to give it back to her tonight", said Janet. "She's to be somewhere out Murray Street."

"She'll not be there for an hour yet. Let's ring some more bells."

Hat in hand she took to her heels down the lane, which by its narrowness invited headlong speed. Her feet pounded on the bare earth, snatched it up, and flung it with its parallels of brick wall racing past her. She felt that she could run for ever; but, if one is a girl, one is always told not to run like that in the street. At the foot of the lane she braced her body back and stopped. There was an inviting door in this street, solid and shiningly grained with a big brass bell, Beside it another crooked lane wound back to the High Street. She pulled the bellknob out as far as the wire would stretch, and then letting go doubled round the corner, followed closely by Janet. Crouching on the ground against the wall Elizabeth advanced one eye and the tip of her nose. There she is!

It would have been more prudent to hold one's breath and remain squatting. But a year ago Elizabeth, who had an accurate eye, had planted a blob of jelly from the height of the parlour window clean on to the crown of the new Sunday hat worn by the very housewife who was now questioning the street outside her affronted door, Their footsteps echoed hollowly as they fled up the lane, and Elizabeth heard screams of indignant recognition following her. She was a little uncomfortable, but buried her uneasiness beneath the bravado of ringing other bells.

As the eight o'clock curfew sounded they walked sedately down the High Street towards the Victoria Bridge, the nightly promenade for the boys and girls of the town. One side of the High Street was more genteel than the other; where primly the shop assistants and clerks walked in twos and threes. But even here groups of mill-girls were skirling in the gutter. On Saturday nights the ploughmen flocked in on their bicycles and then one had to walk in the middle of the road in order to keep one's distance. Elizabeth loved Saturday nights; the shop stayed open until ten, and upstairs there was a picnic supper of twopenny pies which it was her duty to fetch from the baker's. But on week nights she had no excuse for submerging herself in the flood of humanity that washed vaguely up and down the streets, full of undercurrents and perhaps of whirlpools. There were no other Academy scholars on the pavement, and they greeted nobody, until in the narrowings of Murray Street Janet was stopped by Bella Paton, the temporary owner of the Gillespie manuscript.

"How did you like it? Better than yon last one, 'The Captain's Lady'?" Bella's blue eye roved over Elizabeth as she spoke. Elizabeth felt embarrassed. Tomorrow all the shop girls would know that she had read it. What a horrid fuzzy frizzed fringe – curlers of course. Like a mill-girl.

"Elizabeth here makes poetry out of her head", said Janet. "Bet you she could make a better one herself." "Could you really?" Bella Paton's tone was sweet like treacle.

"O yes, perhaps I could."

"My, how clever! See and make one, and give me a shot of it, do!" Elizabeth was uplifted with importance. "O, I'll do that easily."

"She knows all about it, doesn't she? You know what gravy is, don't you, Elizabeth?" Bella nudged her with an elbow. Elizabeth's importance collapsed. She did not know what Bella meant, and she hated her to be familiar.

"I'll have to be going home now, Janet", she said distantly. "I haven't finished my Latin Prose."

"Why, it's not half past eight yet!" cried Janet. "Come out to the Bridge with me, you might."

Elizabeth could not bear to disoblige her friends. She scuffed the pavement with one foot. "All right. Just to the Bridge."

"So long, Bella."

As they walked bridgewards Janet turned to her chum. "Don't you like Bella Paton?"

"N-no", said Elizabeth.

"That's funny" returned Janet, "you like most people."

Typescript among Willa's papers at St. Andrews, ref. No. 91213, with only the chapter numbers as headings, and breaking off exactly as above; though at the foot of a ts. page, leaving it possible that some text was rather lost than abandoned. The story's 'Rossie' is, like the published novels' "Calderwick", recognisably Montrose rather than the actual Rossie, in Willa's day an island village in the mouth of the Montrose (South Esk) Basin, joined to the town by the A92 bridge – RRC

Cakes Not Turned
Willa Muir's Published Novels

Janet Caird

The more one reads of and about Willa Muir, the more one is aware of potentialities unfulfilled. P H Butter has stated that "Her greatest work, I think she would gladly agree, was to make possible the production of [Edwin Muir's] poetry." There are reasons to doubt how "gladly" she would agree, and the picture she herself gives in *Belonging* (pp 162-3) of the difference in their respective working conditions in Hampstead (Edwin in a quiet and secluded study at the top of the house, she downstairs always open to the interruptions of domesticity) does not exactly strike a note of joy. One has the impression she had to struggle hard to find time and space for such work as she achieved.

Her two published novels are *Imagined Corners* (1931) and *Mrs Ritchie* (1933). *Imagined Corners* is a teasing, irritating book, because one is aware of possibilities in it not realised. The prophet Hosea said of the religiously lax tribe of Ephraim that it was "a cake not turned", not cooked through, and the same could be said of *Imagined Corners*. It is written to a classical formula, a group of characters in a small town, "Calderwick", with little beyond it to distract them from their own feelings and passions and resultant actions. Almost the only interventions from forces beyond the control of the characters come from the climate of Calderwick: blinded by a raging blizzard the Reverend William Murray falls into the dock and is drowned; a keen frost sends Mabel Shand and her brother-in-law skating together and allows for the strong sexual attraction between them to surface.

The plot is minimal, a mere framework for the interplay of character, although one might more accurately say 'plots', for there are two distinct groups of characters: the Shand family; and the Minister, William Murray, his sister Sarah and, enduring a severe mental breakdown, their brother Ned. "My first novel had enough material in it for two novels", as Willa Muir herself said. The two groups are awkwardly linked in the action, and on the fringes are characters representing Calderwick: the Misses Watson, two sisters at daggers-drawn with each other; the pretentious Scrymgeours; the Poggis, owners of the fish-and-chip shop, representing the non-respectable side of Calderwick; and Bell Duncan, the girl seduced by Hector Shand prior to the action of the novel.

It opens with a scene in the manse, from which we learn of Ned Murray's mental instability. The main action however centres on the Shand family, John and his wife Mabel preparing to welcome Hector, John's half-brother, and his wife. Black sheep of the family, Hector had been packed off to farm (unsuccessfully) in Canada following his seduction of a local girl. All is now forgiven, he is to have a place in the family flour-milling business and has married a fellow-student at St

Andrews, Elizabeth Ramsay. Just how Hector ever became a student is a mystery. He is depicted as "taking it for granted that books and all that they stood for were beyond his capacity." Elizabeth is passionately in love with him and has to stifle doubts as to their intellectual compatibility, she being idealistic, highly intelligent and interested in books. Not surprisingly, the marriage soon begins to crumble, Hector becomes bored with Elizabeth, flirts with Mabel, hates the mill and finally decides to go away from Calderwick to Singapore, leaving Elizabeth to follow him.

In fact he goes off with his old flame Bell Duncan, but before this happens the Shand family is joined by John's sister Elizabeth, whom John has invited to Calderwick. Whatever significance may be intended by introducing two characters with the same name, the author gets over possible awkwardness by having sister Elizabeth known as "Elise". Elise had run away with a married man as a girl of nineteen, but eventually achieved respectability and a comfortable income by marrying the last of her lovers, Dr Mütze, a German scholar. She does not appear until the last third of the book, and one must ask what exactly her function is. Her arrival, the sophisticated, cultivated, well-to-do woman from Europe, was surely meant to be a turning point in the action. Yet the problem of Hector's marriage has been resolved by the time Elise arrives: he is leaving Calderwick. Her intervention in the Hector-Elizabeth situation is less than admirable, for knowing that Hector is going away with Bell Duncan she helps him to go by giving him money. She does not tell Elizabeth what is going on. Does her undertaking to "look after Elizabeth" justify what is really a betrayal?

Meanwhile the other plot has been tragically resolved, with Ned Murray in an asylum and the Minister dead, drowned in the dock. The book ends with Elise and Elizabeth in a train on the way to Elise's house in the south of France. Elise has come to feel that it might be her *Gebiet* (mission in life? The word translates as 'province') to "clear away stones of prejudice and superstition so that other girls might grow up in a more kindly soil. And Elizabeth would help her…until she fell in love with somebody the exact antithesis of Hector…"

Here comes a weakness in the depiction of character, for Elizabeth, the bright intellectual woman, is weak. One would have hoped to see her realising the hopelessness of her passion for Hector, facing it, coming through the experience "a sadder and a wiser" woman. But no. She is swept away unresisting by Elise just as she had been swept away by Hector. Our last glimpse of her is as her eyes overflow with tears for that worthless man. Hector is quite nasty: self-pitying, deceitful, rude, cruel even without meaning to be, prone to unreasonable jealousy. Just why he has developed so disastrously is not made clear (though there are hints at heredity, and spoiling by his doting aunt). Mabel is successfully drawn: snobbish, selfish, materialistic, shallow – undeserving of her good husband John, a decent, honest middlebrow.

As for the sad family in the manse, Willa Muir was right in realising that here was material for another novel: poor Sarah Murray battling to care for her brothers, Ned in a state of mental collapse, William struggling to be a good pastor and struggling to resolve his own theological bewilderments. The Murray tragedy is awkwardly linked to the Shand story, William attracted to Elizabeth but suppressing his feelings – as she suppresses her nascent attraction to him. She feels guilt for Ned's illness, for she had been present at and had even applauded the disastrous ragging, led by Hector, which had caused Ned's breakdown. This is however revealed, casually, towards the end of the book, and one cannot help but feel that William Murray's fatal accident in the dock was a convenient way of rounding off the Murray tragedy.

Elise Mütze is a kind of Greek chorus, observing and commenting on the characters and action, and a *dea ex machina* swooping down and rescuing Elizabeth from the tangled mess her life has become. She is a cold and detached person, not without arrogance, given some warmth by her grief over the death of her husband. She has at first a condescending attitude towards Calderwick, but while there she is enabled to view her life steadily and view it whole, come to terms with herself and discover her true identity. "She was not to be explained away. She would have been herself even if she had to sing in the streets for a living."

The principal character in the book is in fact the town of Calderwick. With a few deft touches, Willa Muir succeeds in revealing the power of a small close-knit community over its members. The two rebels, Hector and Elise, have their lives shaped by being driven to reject the values Calderwick would impose upon them. Elizabeth, seeking for the truth in a semi-mystical communion with Nature and also trying to be by Calderwick standards a "good wife", fails miserably and has to be rescued by Elise. There is no place in Calderwick for poor, brilliant, mad Ned. Calderwick kills its unorthodox tormented minister by its very climate. The only ones who will survive in the place are the unquestioning people like John Shand, or the calculating materialists like Mabel, and Mrs Scrymgeour the doctor's wife, or the cheerful hypocrites. Willa Muir, on whose native Montrose it is based, depicts Calderwick with cold clarity as the epitome of mediocrity, hypocrisy and self-righteousness.

Mrs Ritchie is also set in Calderwick, and in the character of Mrs Ritchie Willa Muir succeeded in creating a true monster. That she hated her creation becomes clear as the book progresses; in fact, the pleasure the author seems to take in forming her monster produces uneasiness in the reader, for Annie Ritchie is allowed no redeeming feature. In the first chapter, as a child, infuriated by the appearance of her father at the gate of her primary school, she indulges in a daydream: first of all, she visualises her father and sister cowering in snow on an icebound waste, being lashed by hail; and then as slaves cowering before her, as a savage queen with a whip in her hand. The rest of the book is a study of how Annie dominates and destroys her family.

She finds justification for her conduct in a fiercely primitive and fundamentalist form of religion where God and the Devil loom large as vengeful entities. Keeping the Devil at bay justifies her mental and physical cruelty to her children, and her cold callousness to her husband. Her house becomes for her a fortress in which she is supreme tyrant. Outside her fortress she assumes the ultra-conventional role of the upright Christian wife whose husband, as a deacon of the church, must be shown meek respect and whose children, impeccably dressed in Sunday best, sit obediently in the pew. By the end of the book Mrs Ritchie has lost contact with reality: her fixed idea that she alone is fighting against the Devil's malignant influence topples over into insanity, and our last glimpse of her is as she pats the graves of the husband and son she has hounded to death, murmuring, "Poor Johnny... poor John Samuel."

The plot is simple: Annie is a bright child, one of two daughters of a ne'er-do-weel father, in a household kept going by the mother, who takes in washing. Annie's headmaster suggests she become a teacher, but her mother flatly refuses to countenance the idea. Annie as a result ceases to be a model pupil, leaves school at the end of her primary education and goes into service in the home of her Sunday school teacher,

Willa Muir during the mid-1930s
(photo courtesy Irene Abenheimer/Ethel Ross)

Miss Julia Carnegie. There she encounters Bet Bowman, a fellow-servant, a light-hearted careless girl whom Annie regards as an example of worldly wickedness (but who, married as Bet Reid, is destined to play an important part in Annie's life and provide some degree of kindliness in the life of her children, more especially that of her son).

John Ritchie, a joiner, comes to do work in the Carnegie household, and Annie sets out to capture him as her husband. Then, a married woman with a house of her own, Annie is free to develop her own view of life. Within the house her word is absolute: her children, John Samuel and Sarah Annie, are beaten into submission; her husband bullied – at the end of his life she has abandoned his bed and ceased to communicate with him. She is pained to discover that according to the law of succession the house goes to the children. She drives her son, returned from the 1914–18 war, to suicide. Left with her daughter, Mrs Ritchie decides that Sarah Annie is "possessed of a devil" and "a brand to be plucked from the burning." Eventually, by unceasing prying, she drives her daughter from home and is left on her own, a crazed old woman.

The main episodes of the book take place indoors, with one important exception. After learning that her chance of becoming a teacher is over for good, Annie ceases to be the model pupil and becomes one of the group of girls in the playground. This is only a brief interlude: she is humiliated by the girls, there is a violent quarrel, and Annie is once more an outsider. In her hurt rage she runs into the countryside, and climbs on to the wooden bridge over the railway. There she feels something willing her to let go and fall down.

"She clung to the lattice until her head cleared...She gazed at the straight inviolate track of the permanent way...and her spirit followed her eye along promised lines of certainty cutting through the bewilderments of life." Annie lifts her eyes to the sky and sees the setting sun peer at her through a gap in the clouds. "As if a ray had penetrated her, Annie felt that God was looking at her...She knew that until that very evening she had been giving herself to the devil." God, She felt, had singled out Annie Rattray and "beyond the sunset clouds He was thinking of Annie Rattray...God was her Father." This is the crux episode in the book; after this experience Annie is dedicated to fighting the Devil and keeping herself unspotted from the world. On reaching home after her solitary walk, she spends the evening cleaning up her grubby kitchen. Contemplating her sleeping drunken father, she is repulsed by the sight of the hairs on her chest and his stubbly chin. "The devil as every body knew was hirsute all over": body hair becomes for her a sign of Satan.

From now on Annie sees herself as set apart. She has lost her fleeting popularity with her schoolmates, her relationship as star pupil with her teacher is gone for ever. But Annie hugs to herself the knowledge that she is a chosen daughter of God.

Powerful though this description of Annie's "spiritual" experience may be, it remains unconvincing, for we have been given no indication previous to this episode that Annie harboured any ideas of God or the devil. True, she went to Sunday School, where she learnt the Shorter Catechism, but it seems to have been nothing more than a mechanical exercise. Her Sunday School teacher concentrated more on exciting tales of adventures in the foreign mission than on any doctrinal teaching; and while the Rattray family had "sittings" in the church it is impossible to visualise any family discussions of God and the devil in that household. Nevertheless her assumption of the role of chosen daughter of God was a wonderful compensation for her isolation at school.

Annie's realisation of her status as a daughter of God manifests itself in a fanatical dedication to order and cleanliness, and as a housemaid in the Carnegie household she finds full scope for this passion. The theme of the book is established: Annie will spend her life as a domestic tyrant imposing on her nearest and dearest her "God-given" values of order and cleanliness, her weapons against the devil and all his works.

This establishing of Annie's character so early and so fixedly is a weakness in the book, for it gives little room for any development or opening-out of the character. There is little for the reader to discover; there are no surprises, only a reiteration of Annie's determination to fight the devil wherever she finds him. The reader knows how she will react in any given situation – the only question is how far her gloomy fanaticism will carry her. The other characters – her husband, daughter and son – are given little scope for development. Sarah Annie is allowed to show a mild interest in the suffragette movement, and even occasionally makes an effort to answer back to her mother. John Samuel tries to escape by becoming a reporter on the local paper and not a minister as his mother wished; and by enlisting on the outbreak of war. But neither he nor his sister ever breaks the psychological tyranny, which simply crushes husband Johnny into his grave.

It is clear that there is in the book the possibility of a powerful work – a female *House with the Green Shutters* – but at that level the book must be judged unsuccessful. For one thing, the author has not given herself enough space to develop the theme convincingly. Mrs Ritchie looms too large, overshadowing Johnny, John Samuel, Sarah Annie. From time to time their creator indulges in psychological explanations of her characters' actions and attitudes: Annie's isolation in the playground is explained by a page of solemn analysis of the psychology behind children's games; the schoolmaster is described in psychological terms instead of his revealing himelf in action: "If a headmaster is not really supporting the universe, the temple of law and order is an unsubstantial fantasy and he himself is but a mortal man." John Samuel's view of life is carefully explained to us: "A boy who is conscious of some barrier between his emotions and the utterance of them may well believe that he is excluded from all that is warm and intimate in the lives of other people." The effect of these little lectures in psychology is to make the characters appear specimens rather than credible people.

Calderwick is barely sketched, and very little is revealed of what the inhabitants think of Mrs Ritchie, except that the nice ladies who ran the wartime committees made a pet of her, spoke of her as a "character" who was "terribly good at getting things done". Only at the end of the book is this ludicrous opinion shown to be false, when Mrs Ritchie so ill-treats Sarah Annie that she collapses when teaching. Mrs Ritchie is "a devil".

There is little humour in the book, the sardonic description of life in the Carnegie household where Annie is a maid has almost a sneering tone, as if the life of the three sad old spinsters was somehow faintly comic. Throughout the book Mrs Ritchie's fierce religion is treated with an undertone of mockery which detracts from the depiction of its destructive power. There is an ambivalence in the author's attitude to the monster she has created, who is at once fearsome and ridiculous.

The style is undistinguished, the dialogue not always convincing, the book gives the impression of having been written too quickly; an embryo rather than a fully-developed creation. Nevertheless Mrs Ritchie is a remarkable and memorable character, and it is high time the book was reprinted.

The question arises, where did the horrific Mrs Ritchie have her origin? It is very probable that the child Willa, obviously outstandingly bright, would be the odd one out among the children of her Montrose primary school, and might well experience a sense of not being accepted. There is a ring of truth in the description of Annie standing miserably in the playground left out of the "chaos of flying legs and voices" as the other girls play singing games in which her sister takes a leading part. In the holidays Annie plays hopscotch by herself or spends "most of her spare time sitting kicking her legs on a wooden bench." Could the child Willa have spent equally solitary holidays, longing for the time when she would be back in the classroom and outshine them all? Or is Mrs Ritchie an incarnation, an exaggerated incarnation, of Calderwick, of the grim aspect of Calderwick adumbrated in *Imagined Corners*: the Calderwick that sought to impose on all its own rigid and narrow standards of conduct and thought? Is there a link between Mrs Ritchie and the Mrs Grundy of *Mrs Grundy in Scotland*, Willa Muir's study of morality and social conventions in Scotland?

Perhaps if Willa too had had a quiet study at the top of the house, she would have been able to give to the writing of these novels the concentration necessary to work out their possibilities. The recipe is good, but they are not baked through. *Janet Caird*

pitlochry festival '93 theatre

30th April - 9th October

Scotland's most beautifully situated theatre.

Programme changes daily

A FLEA IN HER EAR
by George Feydeau translated by John Mortimer
BEYOND REASONABLE DOUBT
by Jeffery Archer
YOU NEVER CAN TELL
by Bernard Shaw
THE STEAMIE
by Tony Roper
JOKING APART
by Alan Ayckbourn
THE REHEARSAL
by Jean Anouilh translated by Jeremy Sams
LA VIE DE BOHEME
a brand new comedy by John Clifford

plus a series of popular Sunday Concerts.

The theatre is open from 10am for coffee and snacks, art exhibitions and regular craft demonstrations.

For a free brochure call Box Office 0796 472680

Willa In Wartime

Catriona Soukup

I remember the first time I saw Edwin and Willa. After one of the lectures at Czech House, while we were talking and laughing in the hall, I suddenly noticed two people standing apart, watching us. One of them, Edwin, I knew. He had his hand on the elbow of an older looking, white-haired woman, who was leaning on a stick, and he looked happy, proprietorial. She, I thought, seemed slightly on her guard, but also alert and amused. I went up to them. "Don't tell me, Edwin," she said, "this must be Catriona. Now let me see whether I can find Lumir".

Seeing them together for the first time, I was impressed by Edwin's gentleness and vulnerability and of Willa's strength, in spite of her physical infirmity. Only later did I realise that in fact it was Edwin, the survivor, who was the stronger. More certain of himself than Willa, although he never raised his voice, yet vulnerable and easily wounded. He could remember, years later, the exact words used, especially if the criticism or slight had come from a friend. Was it just because he was disappointed in the friend, or was there an element of wounded vanity? Or perhaps a little of both? When we asked him, he shrugged and laughed and changed the subject. Of course Willa knew all about this side of Edwin, and when she took up the cudgels on his behalf she did so to defend him, rather than because she enjoyed the struggle. Edwin achieved resilience and courted timidity (with its attendant shyness). Willa, on the other hand, described herself – correctly – as a "soft-centred creature." She had to overcome this with an aggressiveness which she consciously cultivated. In a letter she wrote to us in 1964, a few years after Edwin's death, and written on his birthday (15th May) she described their relationship: "Edwin was a soft-shell crab and I was his carapace".

Edwin was perfectly content to let Willa come between himself and any adversary. When someone made an offensive remark, Edwin would quickly glance at her, she would smile, and one could sense his relish at her reply. Willa never repeated herself, her irony was always fresh. It was uncanny, I thought, the way that she sensed an attack on Edwin was coming long before anyone else even suspected it. She was provoked by three kinds of remarks: by unfounded criticism of Edwin; by any form of male chauvinism; while anything which revealed pretentiousness or could be interpreted as showing off came a distant third. Edwin suppressed his comments. Willa could not, and would scornfully deride the first two categories; the third was occasionally allowed to pass without comment – just a quick look, her eyes half closed, her lips pursed. We used to say: "They asked for it and they jolly well got it."

When we told her what people were saying about her – and sometimes they were very critical of her outspokenness – she was amused for the most part, but not always. Generally the criticisms were

Studio photograph of Willa Muir taken during the mid-1930s (photo courtesy Irene Abenheimer/Ethel Ross)

trivial and due to misinterpretations or misunderstandings. There were times, though, when her reaction to certain words or opinions was perhaps more acerbic than was called for.

When she felt she needed a shield, she would use a cigarette: first the cigarette holder was taken from her handbag, together with a small plug of cotton wool extracted from the larger ball she carried with her everywhere ("I never go anywhere, outside or inside, without my bag. I don't possess a powder puff, lipstick, mirror or comb, but my bag is never without a packet of fags, my cigarette holder, cotton wool and lighter"). She then stuffed the plug into the holder, took a cigarette, put it into the holder, lit it – and began to talk. Her handbag was, indeed, always beside her, carried from room to room.

She inhaled, leaned forward, and began talking in that unmistakeable East Coast lilt. She was very direct, not rude. Emotion would make her cheeks slowly flush, and darken the normal pallor of her skin. Her hair, smoothed into a bun, was really only a few shades whiter than her complexion. I can see her so vividly – her unusually high forehead under the severely combed-back hair, her aquiline nose, thin lips and a firm chin. The only colour came from her eyes, amused, with large black pupils. One never noticed the colour of the iris.

She was smaller than Edwin, who was already noticeably bent. As the years passed her back became worse, and she was never without pain. She taught us the maxim: "Never walk if you can stand; never stand if you can sit; never sit if you can lie down." She never gave much heed to clothes, so long as they were dark blue or black. A headscarf was her usual protection against the perpetual Edinburgh wind.

Her openness and her refusal to be ignored did not endear her to conventional and "proper" Edinburgh society, where women were expected to take a back seat, to be visible and decorative but silent in mixed company so that the men could hold the floor. After one particularly sticky evening I began to say that I had been reminded of "*Kirchen, Kinder, Kue...*", when Willa interrupted, "it's just the same here. Kirk, Kids, Kitchen."

She refused to conform, and often joined in the conversation with a sarcastic remark, which did not endear her to many. Edwin and she were partners, equals, and Willa did not see why it should be different when they were with other people. So she often used to turn to us, saying that we were the first who were aware of her, and who talked to her when she was with Edwin, and that we were the only *couple* they both loved.

Neither Willa nor Edwin willingly hurt anyone. Willa was as gentle as Edwin, aggressive only when provoked into protecting him, or when somebody had made her feel a non-person. Then her shield and rapier wit would be summoned and her laughter, sardonic, scornful, mocking, would sharpen the precise caustic words – never too many, just sufficient to stab and follow through with a final thrust. Years after Edwin and Willa were dead, we became very friendly with an academic of distinction, a very cultured man; one day, quite by chance, we mentioned the Muirs, and Lumir said that he loved Willa as he loved his mother. To our astonishment the man's expression changed, and where before we had seen gentleness and intelligence we now saw dislike and animosity. At that moment our friendship ended.

Among the lectures Edwin organised was one on modern poetry, comparing poems in English with poems written in the languages of the different National Houses. Lumir drew up an outline for the Czech lectures and went with it to Edwin, to compare notes and to discuss some points. He also told Edwin that he had been forced to use not very good translations and leave out some lovely poems – even exclude some poets altogether – because they had not been translated. Should he, therefore, rely on word-for-word translations? Edwin asked whether he could look at them, and then said that he would show them to Willa. So we paid the first of our many visits to their home. Their comfortable armchairs were covered in spotless, starched off-white material, not improved by Tookampuss's claw-sharpening. Tookampuss was their cat, a nervous, highly-strung creature, darting into the corners of the room when any sudden movement scared her. According to Willa, she was the most neurotic member of the family.

Willa was uncertain of herself, asking (uncharacteristically, as we realised later) how we liked the room, would the loose covers be accepted in Edinburgh, and saying that Edwin had told her that people in Edinburgh were very critical and *proper*. She emphasised the last word with a mocking half-smile. She was recovering from a recent serious operation and walked slowly with a stick, which she also used to emphasise what she was saying. The atmosphere was curiously uneasy.

We were given tea in the usual Edinburgh way: cups and saucers, sugar-bowl and milk jug set on a side table, plates with sandwiches, covered with a cloth, cakes and biscuits, all laid waiting for us. But our hostess's way with the teapot was new to me: my cup was first half-filled, the teapot immediately topped up with hot water – then my cup was filled. She did this for everybody, and then we sat back and enjoyed "our" (as they say in Scotland) tea. It was rationed in those days, and it was only by pouring it out like this, Willa said, that she could still provide a decent cup. But long after rationing was over, whether in Edinburgh, Prague, Dalkeith, Swaffham Prior or London, the ceremony never varied. Lumir used to tease her about her "Scottish thrift".

After tea she gave us her translations. They were faithful to the rhythms, the lengths and the rhymes of the originals. There were about twenty poems in all, and she had translated them in two days. It was an astonishing achievement. Alas, with the exception of a few which were published in *New Writing*, they are lost.

Because of her classical education, she had a firm grasp of grammar, and she also had a gift for languages. It took her a long time to explain grammatical terms to Edwin: what is meant by cases, or by inflection, conjugation and declension. Edwin called it the "torture of words". At first he had found it hard to believe that German, like Latin, placed the verb at the end of a "gothic" sentence. Willa had talked Czech in Prague without paying too much attention to grammar, Edwin would not even attempt it. She had quickly learned enough vocabulary to be able to talk basic Czech. Edwin had none. She warned me that a Czech could easily pronounce half a dozen consonants without any connecting vowels, and when Lumir challenged her she laughingly halved the number – but often repeated the first version. As we left that day, she invited me back to collect the additional translations.

I used to go and see Willa in the afternoons; on my first visit I took Maurice Hindus' book *We Shall Live Again*, and told Willa that I read just about every book on Czechoslovakia that I could lay my hands on. I had never been there, I said, but already I talked about Czechoslovakia as "my home". Willa looked at me silently, and obviously liked what I had said. I had often listened to the Czechs and Slovaks in the Scottish-Czechoslovak House talking about "home" but Willa was the first English-speaker who described Prague and the surrounding countryside to me with a vividness and affection that I still remember.

I told her that I planned to learn Czech after graduating from Edinburgh University, because I wanted to translate Czech writers into English, and I asked her to give me some tips; the few translations from Czech that I had seen seemed stiff and unnatural, whereas (thinking of Kafka) their translations read as novels in their own right. How exactly had they set about it?

Willa read German quicker than Edwin did, so she read the book first. Then, after discussing it, they decided together whether they would translate it. When they decided to translate *The Castle* and *The Trial*, they tore the books in two (though she assured me they didn't normally do this to books). They then tossed a coin to see which half each of them would take. After translating their own part, they exchanged halves, and went through them carefully, correcting each other's mistakes. After the mistakes had been put right, the real work began. One must never, Willa said, depart from the original, but at the same time, one should not stick to it slavishly. It is not so much translation – each language after all has its own syntax – as finding equivalents and transposing them from one language to the other. Sentences must, if necessary, be abbreviated or lengthened, or turned around. Paragraphs and sentences have to "go native" – there should be no trace of the original, foreign construction. A dictionary sometimes helps, but the inner ear must be the final judge which dictates the easy flow of the sestences and eliminates any jerkiness or awkwardness in the prose.

Kafka's disciplined and controlled prose was perfectly adapted to the story he wanted to tell. Any liberties with his text would have been unthinkable. Their only rule, at that advanced stage, was that the syntax of the German text must be adapted to the syntax of the English language. On the other hand, when they began to translate Feuchtwanger's *Jew Suss*, they realised that his style and verbosity ("where one adjective was enough he used five") would have put English readers off. They therefore made their English version by adapting rather than translating this work. When they used what Willa called their "translation factory with conveyor belts" for Feuchtwanger's other works, leaving his style and vocabulary intact, the books were not such a success. "Finally we were sick of Feuchtwanger", and they looked on these translations simply as so much money per page, both in agreement that his work was not literature. Increasingly, as the years passed, it was Willa alone who did the translations, leaving Edwin free for his own writing. When she was able to choose something worthy of her attention it was still "drudgery, but I enjoyed some of it."

Catriona Soukup

A Portrait of Emily Stobo

Willa Muir

What a relief it is that they have all gone, said my wife. *The last two days have been a strain on me*. It is a curious thing that we live for months in this English village without seeing anybody but our two selves, and then suddenly Emily arrives on a Monday, Jess on the Wednesday, and Mary on Friday, so that we have to give up our beds and sleep in the garage, Mary and Emily sharing our bedroom.

It would have been much better if Mary had said nothing about it until after Emily left. I wish she hadn't.

So do I. But I was just as much affected by your saying to me that you felt that Emily had simply come down to pry.

I couldn't help it. I had that feeling very strongly almost from the first night that she arrived here.

Well, it is very strange that I had no inkling of it at all. I welcomed her in good faith. I was genuinely glad to see her. I have always cherished Emily in some peculiar way. She is an indestructible part of my life. I have tried for years to help her by silence and by kindness, and it depresses me to think that kindness is of no avail, and that she has become so completely a creature of her mother. Mary said that obviously she did not believe in me, and that therefore I needn't try to help her... Of course Mary told me because she thought it the only honourable thing to do. Mary was indignant that Emily, who had only just met her, should discuss me with her at all, in my house. But I don't think that matters. My opinion is that Emily came down in perfect good faith, and gradually listened to that little demon of suspicion and jealousy which has been gaining hold on her for all these years. The unsound spot which was in her at eighteen has spread until she is more than three parts corrupted. That is what depresses me most. How can I begin to tell the truth to her when she is looking for a calculating motive behind every word I say?

There is no way of getting at the real Emily. She twists away from you. I once tried, and felt I had failed.

There is no way, in the ordinary sense; that is to say, you cannot get at her by argument or statement. But I have always thought that unconscious influence would have success. I thought she would feel that I cherished her, and was fond of her, and that is why, as I said, I have tried silence and kindness. This visit has been of great interest to me in one respect: it has brought very vividly before me our former relationship, and I can see that even when we were at school together although I trusted her goodwill unreservedly I was always careful of her queer moods; I respected them, and walked very warily until her good humour was restored. I adapted myself to her, and shared her interests, and delighted in her curious freakish sense of humour. I cherished her even then. I can see now that there were whole tracts in me whose existence she cannot ever have suspected. And, of course, that was what hurt me so much when the split came. I mean that she and her mother should think of me as they did, after knowing me for such a long time.

...This visit of Emily's has put it all in a terribly clear light. When Emily and I were at school together her mother paid no attention to her at all. Emily paid very little attention to herself. She used to come to school with yards of braid looping from the foot of a badly hung skirt, and holes in her stockings. Her hair was lovely but it was always untidy. She hated her mother. You know how magnificent her mother still is to look at? She was irresistible then. It used to make me wonder when Emily said she hated her mother, for I used to wish passionately that I had a mother as charming. Emily distrusted her mother, but it never occurred to me to do so. I admired her immensely, even though I knew she neglected her daughter. But in some way Emily was proud of her, too. And when we were up at the University we were both very pleased when Mam came to spend a weekend with us. You know, her rich personality, her rich, warm caressing voice, her jolly laugh, her readiness to find everything amusing and her inexhaustible interest in all our gossip made everything more significant to us. Her vitality stimulated ours. She enjoyed it. She began to think that a daughter was an asset, after all, especially a daughter at a University. She began to send Emily frocks, and Emily wrote her long and detailed letters every week. So when we became chummy with the Bone, of course Mam heard all about it. She came up for a weekend towards the end of our semi year and met him.

Was he good looking at all?

Strictly speaking, no. He was Welsh, and had that queer primitive vitality of Welsh people; he was small and sturdy, and his grey eyes glinted and glittered. ...He was of priceless value to us, for when he was a little drunk he couldn't keep a secret, and told us all the intimate scandal of his particular set. If only these senior men had known that we knew so much about them I don't know what would have happened; but the glory of having so much information which none of the other women had was sufficient for us; we would not have given it away for worlds. The Bone knew that we were to be trusted in that way.

...Mam liked him very much, and was very gracious to him. I remember that weekend. I was just beginning to realise that the Bone liked me better than he liked Emily. It wasn't mere conceit on my part. You know yourself. I was always careful of Emily's feelings, but I knew I was the stronger, and for that very reason I felt obliged to be gentle with her. If I had been a different kind of girl I should have choked her off from the beginning. But we always went out together, the three of us, in great amity. I know now that I sacrificed much of myself in order to keep our friendship intact. It seemed to me more important than anything else. I did not think it out clearly, like that; I was simply conscious of Emily in everything that I did. I let her take the lead in jokes and in ridiculing other people, because she attached more importance to ridicule than I did. I appreciated her jests, and often brought them forward to please her.

Besides, although I was flattered by the Bone's preference I never thought of him seriously as a possible husband for either Emily or myself. He was too small. We towered above him on each side of him. And when one is eighteen that is an insuperable objection! But I was willing to be sentimental, and just beginning to ask myself how I could have a little flirtation without offending Emily. It was only a step from that to the thought that it would be absurd of Emily to take offence, and that I couldn't help it if somebody liked me more than her. If he had wanted to flirt with Emily I shouldn't have minded. So when Mam brought Emily a new evening blouse that weekend, I put on one that my mother had furbished up for me, although I didn't care for it very much. And I remember the surprise in Mam's voice when she said, "Why, Minnie, how nice you look!" It struck me that her tone was peculiar – almost as if she grudged me my looks, as if she had not expected me to look so nice. It struck me, then glanced off me; I thought no more about it.

On that occasion Mam invited the Bone very warmly to spend his Easter vacation in Montrose, and he accepted. Shortly after, he offered to take me out on my birthday – the first time he had asked one of us to go out alone with him – and I went. From then on it was quite tacitly agreed on between us that he was more my friend than Emily's, and after the end of term, before he came to stay with the Stobos, he wrote several times to me, somewhat sentimentally, so that it fell to me once or twice to deliver his messages to Mam. It is strange how at that age one can notice things and yet not notice them. I knew that Mam didn't like it, by her remarks and questions. "How does it come, Minnie, that he wrote to you and not to us?"; but even when I was explaining it away I never thought that she was feeling venom about it.

So the Bone came to Montrose, And just before he came my grandmother fell ill, and I had to stay in the house and nurse her. She died during that week, and I am ashamed to think how I fretted because I could not go down to the Stobos and enjoy myself. I was not going up for the summer term; it was not necessary and my mother could not afford it. I was looking for a temporary job, but it had been arranged that I was to spend at least two weekends with Emily, so I had that to look forward to. It was small comfort, however, for not being able to go down to Union Street and join in the fun. I was able to run down one afternoon before my grandmother died, for an hour; and it dawned on me that something was amiss. I had always been more at home in that house even than in my own, but this time there was a kind of chilling reserve in the atmosphere. The Bone seemed embarrassed. Emily was apparently in one of her bad moods. And Mam was very aloof; no mention was made of my proposed weekends, and when I snatched a moment after the funeral to say goodbye to them, there was no mention of it then. I felt bewildered and depressed. The Bone went away without attempting to see me again. Emily went back to the University in the same way.

A few days later I met an old friend, the organist of a church in Montrose, who I had been meeting for some years in the Stobos' house. I smiled at him, and was astonished to see how gravely he looked at me.

"Did you cut me yesterday?" he asked.

Of course I had not cut him; I had not seen him, that was all.

"I thought," he said, "that you had cut me because of the Stobos, and I should be very sorry to think that you suspected me of any share in it."

My startled face must have shown him that I did not know what he was talking about, and he took me down to a quiet seat in the park, because he thought I ought to know that there was an intrigue against me, Mrs Stobo was denouncing me to all the visitors in her house, to all the people whom I had met there familiarly. He had tried to stem the tide, but in vain. I trembled at first, but I would not rest until he told me what she was saying.

It was in substance what she was to say about me years later. That I was vulgar, not superficially, perhaps, but vulgar in grain, which was much worse. That I had a kind of exuberant vitality but nothing more. That I had no real ability, and was simply a parasite on Emily. In short, that I pushed myself into the limelight, and kept her back, and stole all her ideas. A dreadful picture.

How old were you then?

Just a little more than eighteen.

It must have hurt you dreadfully.

My whole world came crashing about my ears. But my pride came to the rescue – in public, at least. It was a deadly blow to my confidence in myself and in other people. I could not refute such a charge; how did I know that I was really not vulgar? Emily and her mother had known me for all these years, and yet they could say such things about me. The Bone had known me for a year and a half, and yet he could believe them. For he had evidently believed them. I had heard nothing further from either him or Emily. They were both up for the summer term.

Well, I went up grimly to begin my next academic year alone. I took a room by myself. That was an ordeal for me, because the whole University had known of our extraordinary friendship, and I knew they would all be gossiping. I stuck it out, however; I worked hard; it was really a good thing that I was separated from Emily, for I should not have been able to do so much work in her company. But it shows what a strong effect such a vital depression can have on one's body; for a month or two I was ill with the most fearful boils, the last of which prevented me from walking for nearly a week...

[The above fragment from the opening of a novel has been adapted to avoid difficulties of punctuation. Plainly intended to have been the narrator, the husband soon becomes little more than prompt, let alone interviewer.]

Belonging

Lumir Soukup

When I rang the bell a daily opened the door and asked my name. From inside the house I suddenly heard Willa's voice, saying of course I can come in and did the woman think I was going to rape her? I was pleased. This was the old Willa, but a few moments later I was shocked by her appearance: an old, old woman struggling to get up, moving with great difficulty with the aid of two sticks, each step bringing painful sighs. At first she was so bent that her face was hidden, all I could see was her hair, previously so smooth and well kempt, now slightly ruffled and untidy. This time you could see that she had aged. You could see the pain every time she moved, but you never, never heard about it.

After the daily had left, I went to the kitchen with Willa. We prepared a pot of tea, which along with the hot water jug I carried into the familiar sitting room. There she insisted on doing her duty as a hostess, still in the same old manner. Her knuckles, even more swollen and distorted than at my last visit, caused her pain as she poured. There was a difference this time, both the teapot and the hot water jug had to be held in both hands, and it was difficult for her to take the lid off the teapot: the index finger would not bend and she had to press the top of the lid against the side of her index finger with her thumb.

I noticed there was a new cat, 'Popsy', and she told me she had trained it to climb and to be friendly. I was to see it later in London, where it kept her company.

From the kitchen I brought a glass of water to put a bunch of violets in. Willa laughed that their colour almost matched her hair, which, she said, had been done that morning in my honour. Edwin had once told me that Walter de la Mare had asked him to bring a bunch of violets if he visited his grave, and I had remembered that in the morning and had brought two bunches. I asked Willa the way to the cemetery. She told me that Edwin was very near, and insisted on accompanying me, saying "let's be together once again."

We moved very slowly, it really was not far, until we stood in front of the simple dark grey stone with Edwin's dates on it, and a quotation from his poem 'Milton':

His unblinded eyes saw far and near the fields of Paradise.

I just managed to read them. When I put down the violets, Willa choked, "Oh, Peerie B." It was the second time, and the last, that I heard their private language. It was worse than she had foretold in *Imagined Corners*: "everything died – it was intolerable – he had been her measure for so long that without him she was lost – she could only grieve and found no answer." Standing at his grave she told me that Edwin had given up his battle for life. At first she could not bear it, but when she saw his great pain and finally his relief in release from it, "they helped me."

Part of our brain registers our experiences and the events around us. Some impressions and experiences are more vivid than others, and so our "registering" is uneven. This becomes obvious when we want to play back, to recall, the past; and when we want to transcribe the recording. Certain events in our lives are deeply etched and surface by themselves, others require our conscious effort. Yet everything has been registered and nothing is really "forgotten". Some people are more gifted than others in re-playing the tapes of their lives, with total recall, yet no one can wind them back to their beginning and let them play continuously up to the present without jerks and stoppages, and with an equal and constant volume of sound. Willa's total recall was very good.

Edwin wrote his first autobiography (*The Story and the Fable*) in the late 1930s in St Andrews during a very unhappy period, and revised and added to it in the early 1950s when at Newbattle Abbey, again in a strained atmosphere. He spoke of his difficulties in adding to *The Story and the Fable*, in arranging the material, and in its formulation, so that the additions would be in the spirit of the already published autobiography – what to put in, what leave out? Willa started hers, *Belonging*, in the early 1960s at Swaffham Prior, ill, exhausted and unhappy. On various occasions (not all) Willa helped and corrected what she called Edwin's "flights of fancy". When she wrote her memoirs she had Edwin's final, unfinished story beside her. But not Edwin.

From our countless encounters after many events experienced together, I can vouch for Willa's recollections as the more accurate. She was more down-to-earth, a factual, relevant observer; a recorder, whereas Edwin was concerned with atmosphere and the impressions made on him. Occasionally – not deliberately, I hasten to add – he did not see or remember certain things, because he had withdrawn into a dream and a search for formulation. He was an interpreter. To give just one example, Willa's operation and recovery as described in *Belonging* (p207) and in *An Autobiography* (pp248–9), one almost wonders whether they were writing about the same event. Knowing Willa, I believe her unsentimental account. She was, as I say, a recorder.

The autobiographies have to be read together, because they complement one another. Often Willa included incidents which Edwin omitted. Times and facts and places, some missing in Edwin's recollections, are more accurately given by Willa. The acute critic of literature is silent about the less-than-perfect deeds of his fellow writers, Willa does not gloss over their shadier sides. When one reads Edwin's account of some of his friends, and then reads Willa's, one has difficulty in believing that they are writing about the same people. Ever shy of betraying his feelings, Edwin in his book speaks of Willa as "my wife"; Willa, direct as always, uses the more intimate "Edwin" throughout.

Edwin's additional chapters, apart from small inaccuracies, are uneven. They lack firmness of thought and judgment, which is surprising because neither then nor at the very end was his mental capacity affected by time or circumstance. The only explanation, and perhaps excuse, is that they were written hastily, and also that he could not really concentrate, whether due to difficulties and differences with the administrators of Newbattle Abbey, or more likely because he felt that his real writing was his poetry.

It was a pity that Willa felt morally obliged to write *Living with Ballads* (published 1965), for which Edwin had received a financial grant from the Bollingen Foundation. When he died the book was not even in its early stages, and Willa took it over, writing a solid academic work which could have been written only by someone with a complete grasp of the subject in all its diverse aspects. Giving an inventive classification and certain indications, it is still overlooked and neglected. Writing it was, I know, a useful and even necessary therapy, but her heart was not in the work. She had already conceived the idea of writing about her life with Edwin.

Just as in his unhappy period shortly before and after the beginning of the war Edwin turned to the days of his childhood happiness and started to write *The Story and the Fable*, so Willa, visibly broken in body but even more bruised in spirit, longed to write of their forty happy years together. As she was organising her ideas and subjects for *Living with Ballads* into a scholarly arrangement of different chapters, she began to jot down some thoughts that were later used in *Belonging*. In a letter of 9 February 1964 she wrote that she had started the fourth chapter and was writing for some details.

I knew that the wound was too raw for systematic writing, the necessary detachment, if it could ever be attained, was still absent. In some instances it was not attained due to exigencies of time. *Living with Ballads* had far too complicated and vast a range for one person to encompass alone, the more so since Willa was hurt, ill, in constant pain and of advanced age. Also, she was forcing herself to concentrate on writing against the dictates of her heart, allowing herself only short intervals for the planning and writing of the work she considered – rightly – the more important. When it came to the actual continuous writing of *Belonging*, age, the efforts of past years, constant pain and ill-health (attacks of bronchitis as well as crippling arthritis) all took their toll.

The aspects of the past that were clear were put down first. Others were recalled with effort, and these fresh notes had to be sorted, along with the older ones, and put into sequence. Only then could she start systematic writing, beginning with the year of their first meeting and continuing up to Edwin's death. She knew that the writing was uneven, and – as she later admitted – that certain passages should have been omitted. They were taken from her diaries.

"Listen what I have found in my diary", she wrote in a letter, and one could hear her chuckling. Then it was left in the draft, never to be corrected. There was the insidious fear that she might be unable to finish it, hence some hastily written sentences and paragraphs. Always there was the hope that, later, she would be able to correct and change the passages that she herself knew needed rewording – we need only look at her novels to know how she could write. There were moments of despair when a viral infection made her "nearly blind", and for a long time afterwards she had to use a large magnifying glass. She told me that she was frightened of starting the rewriting, and of leaving perhaps an unfinished manuscript. If only *Living with Ballads* had not taken so long, *Belonging* would have been different. It would not have been "written by a tired old woman" (letter, 22 December 1967).

The above is not offered as excuse, but rather as explanation. *Belonging* needs no apology, it was written as a testimony to a unique partnership between two true lovers, "the weaving together of two lives without either domination or subjection" (letter of 15 May 1968, Edwin's birthday). Edwin had written many love poems to Willa, finally inscribing a dedication of his *Collected Poems* to "Willa". It was now Willa's turn, *Belonging* is her long poem, the Story written in prose, and "Dedicated to Edwin Muir with love."

During those years and for years to come, Support and practical help came from a comparatively new friend, the poet Kathleen Raine, whose wise advice and guidance and totally unselfish care Willa gratefully accepted. She moved to a London flat, finally escaping from Swaffham Prior, where she had been alone and unhappy.

> Kathleen Raine (who nearly came and kidnapped me) has offered me the semi-basement flat of her Chelsea house, where I shall be,
> (7 August 1963)

> Please don't be sorry for me, I am lucky to be here, in Kathleen Raine's home, which is full of people friendly to me, not to mention Kathleen herself ... She is a darling, and very kind to me ... I have recovered from the dreadful state I was in when I first came here ... One of the nice things about my being in London is that from time to time I see old friends, and always have intelligent conversation at hand. I go upstairs to dinner parties in Kathleen's rooms so not being able to go about London doesn't matter much. (9 February 1964)

When Willa's biography is eventually written, her letters will show how Kathleen Raine "preserved my sanity". She called her fellow-writer "my guardian angel", and said she could never be thankful enough to her for saving her.

In 1968, during the "Prague Spring", I had to go often to London and was able to visit her (so much happier in her London flat) more frequently. I had by then known Willa for over twenty years, and had for a long time felt that I would like to hear her answer to one question, even though it was superfluous, because we both knew it. Had she never, even for a moment, regretted the loss of her independent career? Surely she must have had her own ambitions, after her brilliant degree and the subsequent opportunities for her to enjoy an academic life, or after their arrival in London? She gave me her characteristic piercing look, laughed and raised her hand to stop me, but I asked her to let me finish. I insisted on putting the question, for the record. And where, I added, did her views on a woman's role fit in?

> You know the answer. My career was Edwin. I devoted my life to Edwin and I knew what I meant to Edwin, and he knew what he meant to me. We both remained true to each other, and to ourselves as well. That is what our life was, a daily tryst, and his poems are the fruits of it. I asked, are they only *his* poems?
>
> You know how susceptible Edwin was to criticism and to suggestions from other writers. Sometimes I had to fight against alterations. I was the first to hear and read his poems. How could I have kept quiet? However, what good would it do to go through them line by line...? But let me be absolutely clear: it was Edwin who conceived, formulated and wrote the final version of every poem. They are *his* poems.

Willa continued, as always reading my mind: "My own writing..."

"You didn't really give it a chance", I interrupted.

"My own writing", she repeated, "could never have been as important as Edwin's, and I'm glad I recognised that early on."

I told her that I knew, Edwin had told me many times, that she had "slaved" over translations of books she did not really like, in order to make it possible for him to devote *his* time to writing. Did she never consider that Edwin was, in a way, "*primus inter pares*", and that she might be thought of as "*seconda*" in their relationship, even though we both knew this was neither true nor just?

"Does it matter?"

I saw she was getting tired, and that our conversation was bringing back too vividly not only memories of joy, but also reminders of loneliness. It was time to go, and seeing her, half-sitting, propped up in the bed, I thought it was the right moment to tell her what had been in my mind for years. "Do you know, Willa, the words Edwin used, when he talked about the first months of your life together and his hesitation about leaving a secure job in Glasgow, after you had persuaded him to start a new and different life in London? He said, 'Willa rescued me'. And in Dalkeith, describing his break-down after his experiences in Prague, he told me 'Willa saved me.'"

She deserved to hear about Edwin's love and gratitude.

Lumir Soukup

Vuyelwa Carlin

Shah Jahan in Prison

They have sunk tiny mirrors into the wall,
here – for my happiness;
silvers, facing, in the sandstone's deep lattice;
– see it, hunch of shimmers,

coddle, white and jewelled,
for the holding for ever of her little
softness of ash. – I grew old

watching the moulding of it, dove
crouched on secret dark, impenetrable
love-work. I remember, dusty days,

walking in the courtyard of the blazoners,
where year on year they shaped
the petals of bloodstone, jade, agate: milk murk

ghosting the intent marblemen
where they glossed and cut. – I planned,
if years were given, a gloomstone twin,

rich crow, my dust's
black carcanet: had cleared, sketched
the sand – that pinkness, there, rose-smudged

with their cells, delicate-hands. – Not for me
– earthmouth, blooded – to share
the cradle of her heart, that

most pure powder: – some wind-
dwindle, soon, ash-roam: – meanwhile I dream, gaze
in this little round, my pride, grief's slake

almost: impeccable block on block, slow-
gouged, painfully pressed
with a thousand days' precision
of gem-flake – leaf, and bud, and calyx.

Cattle Rushing

The high road and a high moon:.
the cattle, woken,
stranged with silver,
ran, a wild herd,
all the long field: the bull,

even, his ponderousness
of day left by, legged it,
ashen thunder,
dense neck swaying, amid
his silent silver women intently.

Bulls

– And bulls – pale mountains,
blondweight – they have filled
– slow, still, secretly wild –
this summer, these fields. One,
chivvied pile, blanched lumberer,
treads a green lane unobjecting –
torpid quicks, all swallowing,

of a curd sea; dull billower,
wan gleamer, opacity. Or solid
as marble, emperor, unmistakable
even from far, one sits, block
of pallor, hugeness of Carrara.
His eye, dawn-pink, half hid:
he is old chalk hills: meek, mad.

Darksmith

His great hammering hands
beat delicacies – such thins –
black wandering filaments: – he runs,

leaps, screams
– his dog scampering silently by –
the village rings
with his fierce dreams.

In summer he softens, sweating
in heart-crimson
among his iron webs: – dead winter

saddens: he strides
with his old scuttling dog the bleak,
bleak white hills, sobs.

The Fisherwoman

I fish deeper than most,
barb the nameless
– saucer eyed, centuries-blind
strangeness.

From fathered littleness to
this gaunting: –
over our greys and purples
I go jaunting,

chillblood; am a wind-cage,
whirligigged through, cold
as the extreme water:
where I grapple and toss

is even beyond bird-laughter.
– I netted his old clay,
the death-night;
gently he danced

to deepbite. – Raw with rollick
of salt – my winy sip –
I hook him up thousandly,
jewel-lip.

Vuyelwa Carlin

Roy Allen

Time's Nightmare

Lost in an endless sea of time,
discarded on an island,
steel and sear,
whose outer reefs,
cold razor-wire,
preclude escape...
From all around
deep ocean waves of years,
months high,
in serried ranks
and perfect metronomic pace
roll in and, finding shallows,
start to break.
White foaming days and weeks
appear to dash my hopes
with unrelenting hours
and, as the undertow of countless minutes
drags me screaming to despair,
the drowning seconds
suck my final breath away.

Come to the Zoo

Come to the zoo and there,
in stinking cages, ten by seven,
watch as insensate beasts
with haunted, sunken eyes,
unfocused stare,
pace, aimless, back and forth.
Through peep-holes peer and pry,
to see them urinate or sleep,
all privacy and pride expunged,
displaced by hopelessness and fear.
When will you realise
it's punishment enough
to keep them from their family and kind.

Home Guard

I will not bleed
upon another's land.
I need no foreign field
to make my final stand.
Within my sight
within my arms,
within my care
are all that's worth the fight.
Here is my home.

Disappointments

How quick life's die
flips o'er from six to one.
Such fleeting hints at fortune
are no more, no less.
Thus certainty is paradox,
our heartbeat flutters,
gambles, makes it race,
and losing faith demands
its debt of blood.

Roy Allen

Antonia Dodds

Quarry

They were a cold people here;
even their loving was cold,
black as water, fragile as stone
swift as her hands upon the harp.
If you sit with me among the shards
you will sense this too;
and the black shags brooding
on the gully's edge.

When the Iris Bloom

Sometimes the truth is to be found
In the untied threads before the story's end,
The cloud before the parting of the sun;
And if I leaned my head against you,
Only the wind binding our hair,
Then take me in before you let me go,
As the waves move up upon my waking shore.

The mountains rise heavy from the sea,
With their floating heavy grace: this quick mist
Blinds my eye as much as your touch liberates;
Or shifts the shifting ocean into whose greyness
I summon islands, the distant silent sailing ship
Resolves its perfect self to pass away.
And I think that if I walk enough into the rain
The sun will come.

Words are not the only way
If you were here with me now it would be different
I would touch you where I touched you not before
My voice sounds different when I speak alone.

So many beginnings I have seen
Growing their green way up towards the sun
And I will have to let such others go
Across the water
But I will be here when the iris bloom.

I'm scared to move my ghost,
Shake the glass beads from out his eyes,
Touch the flesh that will move away,
Allow more than five words from his lips.

There is a hidden brightness in the air,
Spring has come if not to me,
There is a weariness in certain words,
And I will be here when the iris bloom.

Maunday Thursday

This is not a night for sleep
On such a night as this the moon rose,
Grey with anger, laying her light across the water
In silence – the bloody cross was here:
It was you, and I, and the empty cymbal.
Too much of the crowd is in my heart.

It was you, and I; and the sickness
In her covered head. This is a healing place,
This midnight.

Alastair Dunnett

Bridal

All time was made for all mankind.
    This night for you and me.
There are some bonds that only bind,
    And some that set men free.
I reach my hands to you, and find
    The chains of liberty.

So gyved, we double our delights,
    And halve the God-sent woe;
And endless joys, in days and nights
    Will end when He says so –
But briefly. After death's short rites
    Beyond the sun we go.

Nae Grief for the Makars

Unheeding *anno domine*
    Nae mortal thocht *conturbat mi* –
Delighting yet in Fate's fell sorties
    I hae nae time for *timor mortis*.

For me's but ae *modus vivendi* –
    Frae low-doon glens up-by t'ascend aye,
Spier frae Ben Darien like Cortes,
    And hae nae troke wi' *timor mortis*.

Bringin oot the Bards

William J Rae

Mulgrew the magpie wis frettit kind owre his son, Mungo. Wi Mulgrew bein ane o the heid bummers in the Cooncil o Magpies, it didna seem fittin that the laddie should be a muckle sumph athout ony glisk o ambition.

"Wad you nae like tae be a leader o birds like me?" he wad spier at him.

"We canna aa be leaders", Mungo wad reply.

Mulgrew wis sae fashed aboot the haill thing that he even spak tae Maxwelton the Bard aboot it ae day.

"The laddie aiblins needs a whilie tae mature", said the Bard. "You shouldna push at him."

"Maybe no," replied Mulgrew, "but I feel he's needin somethin tae spark him aff a bit."

Maxwelton thocht for a meenit, syne said: "You could pit him tae ane o thae Creative Bird Sang courses. Man, juist aboot aabody's a poet or teller o tales nouadays. Dae you ken this? Whaun I wis a laddie, wi my mither haudin at me tae be a makar, it wis the kind o ambition that made a chiel an ootlin. A body wis like tae be lauchit at by his freends. But the day, there's a poet in ilka secont or third nest, and maist o them aspire tae teach Creative Bird Sang."

Mulgrew wis auld-farrant kind and, like Maxwelton's mither, thocht it wad be braw for his bairn tae be a poet. Sae he didna tak muckle tent o Maxwelton's rantins.

"Man, Mulgrew, makars are born, nae made. The gift maun be in a chiel. You canna expeck the Muse tae gie her favours tae aabody."

But Mulgrew wis already mindin on his freend, Menzies, wha had retired frae the Cooncil o Magpies, because he wis peyed mair worms for entertainin fowk wi his stories. Shairly he wis the chiel tae teach Mungo Creative Bird Sang. Aye, and whit wis mair, Menzies had takken tae bein a poet anaa nae langsyne, albeit a body didna get peyed sae mony worms for recitin poems. Aa the same, he believed it cairried mair prestige.

Sae Mulgrew niver heard Maxwelton's last words: "There's naething but upstart craws dressed in oor feithers nouadays", for he tuik awa like stoorum tae visit his auld freend Menzies.

He tellt him whit he wantit, but Menzies got haud o the wrang end o the stick.

"Sae you want tae tak ane o my courses? Mulgrew, I'll suin mak you the maist renounit bard amang us magpies, mair kenspeckle nor yon Maxwelton. You'll be faur mair cried oot nor you are in the Cooncil."

"But it's nae for mysel. It's for my son, Mungo."

Menzies wis a bit pit oot. He'd heard Mungo wis a gey sweerbreeks. But he said it wadna maitter. He could teach onybody. Forbye he wisna for lossin a customer. He had fund you were peyed mair worms for teachin Creative Bird Sang nor you were for practisin it.

"Can I bring the laddie tae you the morn's morn?" spiert Mulgrew.

"Aye that'll dae fine. I think that fits in wi my ither appeyntments."

Young Mungo wisna sair pleased aboot it though.

"But faither, I dinna want tae be a poet or a storyteller", said he. "I'm blithe tae be the road I am."

Ah weel, he micht hae spared himsel the argie-bargien. Mulgrew's mind wis made up and that wis aa there wis aboot it. Sae neist mornin Mungo fand himsel at the nest o Menzies, the teacher o Creative Bird Sang.

"Nou, Mungo, frae this verra meenit you're a poet," the chiel declaurt.

"Hou can I be a poet frae this verra meenit? You haena taught me ocht."

"Oh, but I hae", said Menzies. "For the first thing you need tae ken is that a body's a poet gin he but cries himsel ane."

"I canna see that", objeckit Mungo.

"Weel, luik at it this road", exclaimed the teacher. "Gin you want tae be thocht o as a doctor, you maun pit up a sign sayin you're ane."

"But shairly it wad be for ither fowk tae say whether I'm a poet or no."

"Niver! You winna get onywey gin you're aa blate and modest. And anither thing – tae be a poet in this countra, you maun threep on hou warkin-class you are."

"But I'm nae. You ken fine my faither an me hae niver dane ony sair darg, wi him bein on the Cooncil and me bein unemployed."

"Daesna maitter", cried Menzies. "You'll niver compete wi aa thae speugs an stirlins, thae bards frae Glesca and Embro, athout passin yoursel aff as a proletarian. Yon's whit maist o them dae, onywey."

Mungo didna seem convinced. Shairly Maxwelton wis a kenspeckle makar and he'd niver made oot he wis warkin-class? But he said nocht.

"Whit's mair," threepit Menzies, "your criticisms o life in this countra will cairry mair wecht that wey."

"But I dinna want tae gang criticisin onything", objeckit Mungo.

"Whit? Nou, hear this, as the Yanks say: you'll niver get onywey athout findin aathing wrang wi society, this countra and the haill warld."

"But aa I want is a quait life", said the pupil.

"Niver. As a poet you maun hae whit they cry 'a divine discontent'."

"I dinna ken aboot 'a divine discontent'. Frae whit you're sayin it souns mair like haein a chip on the shouder. I dinna want tae deave aabody wi compleynts."

Menzies wad fain hae beaten his pow on the waas o the nest. This loon o Mulgrew's wis faur frae bein guid Creative Bird Sang material.

"Weel, weel", he declaurt. "Gin you dinna miscaa aathing aboot the countra, fowk'll say you're nae brainy. Nou a bard here maun, abune aa, show he has harns."

"I dinna ken gin I'm qualifiet in that respeck, onywey."

"You could aiblins carry it aff, laddie, juist by seemin tae be cliver. Nou, gin you winna be a revolutionary, there is anither wey o appearin tae be cerebral, and that's niver tae say onythin simple-like or direck. You maun aye hae fowk chavin tae mak oot whit you mean."

"But is that nae real difficult tae dae?" spiert Mungo.

"It is for some chiels," replied his teacher, "but wi practice you'll suin manage it. Ane o the tricks is tae speak o ae thing in terms o anither, like sayin 'the waa is a perlicket o green cheese!'"

"Whit daes that mean?"

"It daesna mean onything, but it souns profound-like, daes it nae? And you see, I did it by speakin o the waa as if it were the mune. Ken this, laddie, I'm gettin richt up tae't, sae I am."

"But, wi respeck, wad it nae be easier tae seem gleg and sharp by bein humorous or witty?"

"Guidsakes no!" cried Menzies. "Yon wad niver dae ataa. Gin you uis humour or wit in this countra, they'll say you're nae a serious poet. You maun aye be critical or doolie."

"And whit aboot luve poems then?"

"Weel, you micht try your hand at ane or twa, and I'll nae say but whit the ordinar fowk michtna appreciate them. But they winna cut muckle ice wi the intellectuals. You'll nae win faur wi them by sayin your luve is like a reid, reid peony. And anither thing – the intellectuals luik doun their nebs at rhymin poems. Owre cosy for this coorse modern warld, they say. Mind, fower letter words are aa richt, sae they are."

"But should a body nae be makkin poems tae please the ordinar fowk, onywey?" spiert Mungo.

Afore Menzies could answer, twa young magpies flew in aboot. He luikit relieved-kind.

"I'm sorry, Mungo", said he. "Here are my neist twa pupils, sae we'll hae tae leave it at that the day. You'll be back at the same time the morn?"

"Maybe aye and maybe no. We'll see whit my faither says."

As Mungo flew awa, he heard ane o the young magpies sayin: "The acorn o justice is smilin tangentially."

"Braw", cried Menzies. "That's the kind o thing I'm efter."

Back hame Mungo wis quizzed by his faither.

"Hou did you get on, son?"

"Nae bad, faither."

"Daes Menzies think you'll mak a poet?"

"Aye, gin I become a revolutionary, he says."

"Oh my, but we canna hae the son o ane o the Cooncil o Magpies gaein aa bolshie-like. I see I'll hae tae gie this Creative Bird Sang business some second thochts."

Mungo tried tae luik disappeyntit.

"I could aiblins get you on a Social Wark course insteid", said Mulgrew.

Mungo thocht hard, syne had a bricht idea. Glowerin straicht at his faither, he declaurt:

"Ambrosially skirled the revitalised dodos whirling fortuitously."

William J Rae

THE CEILIDH HOUSE

The **H**igh **S**treet wis yince a hub o music, poetry an' talk.
The **C**eilidh **H**ouse pits back that tradeetioun.
Folk nichts – poetry nichts – an aye-bidan come-aa-ye

ilka nicht o the week a new stramash!

Cleik yer pals in fur a pint or a dram. Ye'll hae a waarm walcome.

Eldritch neuks and crannies fur smaa foregaitherings
Cellar haa fur middlin-scale occasiouns

The Ceilidh House, 9 Hunter Square, Edinburgh EH1 1QW
Heid Wanger: Cy Laurie
Tel 031-220 1550

William Imray

Sang For Yule

Yule's amon's, a braa bairnie,
    her een kindlin the winters day!
Yule's amon's, a blyth bairnie,
    her laach thaain a winter's wae!

Wi Yule tae cheer's, lat's hain oor fears
    for this and that, for thon and tither,
the young forget his eydent fret
    tae hae the better o his brither,

the aald be fasht nae mair gin manse be
    buskit for them ayont the mune;
but raise a glaiss tae BRAA BAIRNIES
    THAT WILL BE, AS THEY AYE HAE BEEN!

The Warrant Sale

They hae taen the weidow's ashet,
    her aacht-day clock and aa,
and the wallie dugs and her guid man's fiddle
    that hung on the ingle waa.

"O I never lookit for muckle
    frae thon greed-wude government men:
but nou I hae seen baith neebor an frein
    mak my misfortune their gain!

"They ha gien ten pence for my ashet,
    my dugs gat twenty the pair;
my aacht-day clock it gaed for fifty,
    and the fiddle for no muckle mair!"

She'd barely said her sayin
    when a van draas up i the street,
and she spies a curran freins an neebors
    come laachin in at the yett.

"O we s' wyte we 'greed a price, guid lady,
    and whae wad buy ilk thing;
and we perswadit the lave, lady,
    tae haad abeich frae biddin.

"Yet we wad hae ye ken, lady.
    it wisna frae disdain
we gied sae little for aa your gear,
    nor yet for greed o gain.

WARRANT SALE

STANZAS 1-4

1. They hae taen the weidow's ashet, her aacht-day clock & aa, & the

walie dugs & her guid man's fiddle that hung on tho ingle waa.

STANZAS 5-7

5. 'O we s' wyte we 'greed a price, lady, & whae wad buy ilk thing; &

we perswadit the lave, lady, tae haud abeich frae bidding.'

STANZA 8

Thir peitiless men sall come tae ken & thon wife wha heidit affairs, there's mair nor

troke in the hairts o folk, tho' there's little else in theirs! There's little else in theirs!

Song setting by William Imray

"Here's back your ashet, your wallie dugs,
    your aacht-day clock an aa!
Here's back the fiddle your guid man played!
    Lat it hing aince mair on the waa!

"Thir peitiless men sall come tae ken
    and thon wife wha heidit affairs
there's mair nor troke in the hairts o folk,
    though there's little else in theirs!"

Biggit In

First the rowp an syne the flittin
    neist the carrie wierin dene
'n naethin left tae buy a new ene –
    stene bi stene ye're biggit in.

Ne'er a week but sees its liftin,
    nou a neebor, nou a frein,
hist-ye-backs but fyower tae heed them –
    stene bi stene ye're biggit in.

Crochlie queets an haaspipe's craichle.
    blaither bursn or ye s' win ben,
haans that shak an shanks that buckle,
    stene bi stene they s' bigg ye in.

Fingers on the string carfufflin
    raivellin reels ye thocht they'd ken,
mairch ill mynt, straspey forgotten
    stene bi stene are biggin y' in.

Usquebae mair pyne nor pleisur,
    hochmagandie's hotch lang gene,
muckle speak a waefu strissle –
    never ony wint o stene.

Syne – a stoun that's nae for tholin,
    brakkit bene that winna menn –
life's companioun tene afore ye
    makes a stene the wecht o ten.

Kyn kin syne, concernit for ye,
    (kynlier aye fin gear's tae win)
senn y'awaa an sell the hoosie,
    hae ye braalie biggit in

"faar" say they "ye're connacht rarelie!
    Jeist lik bein a bairnie again!"
Bairns hae warlds o breerd aboot them,
    nae a stookin waa o stene,

nocht tae dee but glower afore ye,
    music that's but maddenin din,
freins tae see ye fain tae lea ye,
    glaid 't's nae them fa's biggit in.

"Spik o times gene by!" they s' tell ye;
"Ye're wi fowk ye kent lang syne!"
Fowk fa sit there dowff an dosint,
    deif's the stene that's biggin y' in?

"*Think* o pleisurs past!" they say syne.
    Wytefu thochts is aa ye ken,
deed ill vrocht an word ill spoken
    biggin in their ain bit stene.

E'en the glaiks eence gart ye glorie,
    rises tene o beasts an men –
peity turns them aa tae scunner
    and anither huntle stene

for the waa that's aa ye think on,
    coontin holies left for stene,
sizin quantities tae steek them
    or the biggin-in be dene.

Had ye seen fut lay afore ye,
    Samson's roadie I s' wyte ye'd tene,
haalit the haill bield doon aboot ye,
    bedd'n for nene tae bigg ye in.

Wintin nou the means tae wark it,
    'thoot the will tae taickle't e'en,
ye s' rehearse yer rochest curse yet
    t' hansell ben their himmist stene.

                    William Imray

rab fulton

hints

some setirdays
wherr ah used tae staye
asian shoap keepirs
pull thir shuttirs doon early
n staun at thir doors
watchin thi passin fitba fans

here n there oan
skyes aye drookit coastline
lang black fingurs
o haurdind lava
streetch doon
intae thi sea

hints o past
noise   violence
destruction   fire

skye poem

ablow grey lift,
atop grey-green sea,
sgeir dubh intrudes.
muckle fur a crag,
peerie fur an eilean,
waves crash white
owre its stuntit
squattin black.

oan still nichts,
west abune ardnish,
tintit yella n brichter
than ony starn,
jupiter kinkles bonny.
in sheer daurkness,
its ripplin reflection,
thi ainly sign
thit hush'd,
allt linnidal still flows.

sae brief a lanscape;
sic ferly contrasts;
nicht, day,
dreich, clear,
winter, summer,
pain, joy,
n mair, oan infinite
in mony combinations. yit,
scarcely a mile
ever separates
jupiter fae sgeir dubh.

aye ablow death,
aye atop birth,
man, whit rerr place this!

thi heron

oan a sma low
brig owre thi kelvin
ah stoapt n tawkt
briefly tae a lass
wae thick rid hair
thick green stockins
thick spectacle lenses
n a nothrin voice
thin n sweet

tellt mi
she'd been
watchin thi heron
fur quite a while
n he hudnae yit
moved fae yon
bough thit ercht
fae thi river
near its richt bank

so ah jyned
thi vigil
gowpin
hopin yon
erlish beast wid

streetch its muckle
black tap wings
ripp thi air wae
its lang grey
heavy talons
snap its sharp
vulture beak
open n shut

thi heron
watcht iz

n preened
itsel
in a gey
gallus waye

its boady
styd stock still
its talons
motionless
ainly its lang
heid moved

motioned by
its flexible neck
it checkt unnir
a wing oar peckt
it its pale, wae
black pokerdots, chist
oar twistit owre
its shoodir
tae groom its back

aa thi time
its form held
in unco balance.
even thi waves
owre its a-whummle
image moved slo
n humble n canny

it lookt at iz
geed its wings
a shak – we waitit
it look it iz

n simply fluttirt
fur a few feet
doon tae thi river
n quick

wiz gane
leayin air
insects n iz
spluttrin in its wake.

breacais iosal 5 april '91

thi bothys waarm enuch
fur us tourists,
thi coal hums n spits,
andrae n norbert
ha'e kaffee n plätzchen,
ah ha'e purridge n broth,
aa we need noo
is a better reception oan
thi black n white portable.

pairt ae thi roof
is corrigaitit plastic,
thi rain drums doon,
lood n constint,
near droonin oot
thi unitit nations' bletherins
aboot thi kurdish crisis.

ootside thi bothy,
doon at thi shore,
ur remnints ae auld dwellings,
boulders slowly losin shape
neath saftnin seaweed,
thi former tenints
lang syne gane,
n ony ghaists left
widnae recognise this rubble.

ah cud write this waas
back intae shape,
create imaginary people
fur cerebral hames.

ach naw,
whits thi point,
tides n seaweed,
n rain n wind,
wirds alane
cannae stoap
thir inevitability.

rab fulton

The Preparation of Meat

Maggie Stephen

Poultry

Liz: I dinnae ken how you've no been here before. D'ye no want to look after your body, or what? This aerobics business'll pull yer arse in, anyway.

Jenny: As long as that's all it does, I'm game. I cannae be doin with all that posin lark. Look at her ower there. Who does she think she is?

Liz: Och, you dinnae know what's good for you. Did ye no see they beefcakes up the stair? There's nane o them's gonnae fancy you when ye're all saggy like that. Flab's no attractive, ye ken.

Jenny: A wee bit o fat never did me nae harm. This place is more aboot bein vain. I came here to exercise, no to get picked up. You'd better behave the night, right? I'm sick of havin to dig you out of holes.

Liz: Shut up moanin, the music's started.

Beef and Pork

Dave: I dinnae feel like doin too much o these weights the night. There's a pool and stuff in the suite doon the stair. D'ye fancy headin doon there in aboot half an hour?

Glen: Aw, come on! If we're only spendin half an hour in here, why no just get straight doon the pub afterwards? You're takin this all a bit too seriously for my likin.

Dave: Aye, an ye can tell where your interests lie. Look at that paunch!

Glen: What?

Dave: Yer belly, eedyit!

Glen: Get lost, you bloody muscle man you think ye are! I can still pull them in, even with a bit o a belly! Natural charm!

Dave: Is that right? You dinnae exactly look fit for the chase noo. Yer face is beetroot. Haen a spot o bother?

Glen: Na. I'm just needin a drink. An a look at the women an all!

Dave: Fit women doonstairs, I tell ye. No that they'd be interested in the likes o you.

Glen: Ye think so? Well, we might have to see about that.

The Marinade

Dave: So, do youz come to this pool often then?

Liz: Whit sort o a corny line's that? Me an my friend come here three times a week for the aerobics. Are youz fae up in the weights room?

Glen: Aye, that's us. Dave thinks he'll build himself up by eating six raw eggs for breakfast! That's crap, boy, ye just need six pints for breakfast! I bet you ken that, eh hen?

He shouts this to Jenny, who is swimming. She ignores him.
Whit's wrong wi yer pal?

Jenny: There's nothing wrong wi me. I'm just doin what I came here for. That's exercise, in case you didnae know.

Glen: D'ye no have awfy trouble at the aerobics wi all that bouncin up an doon?

Dave kicks him under the water.

Jenny: What?

Dave: Dinnae mind him. He's no exactly bulgin in the brain department.

Glen: Aye, but there's other places to bulge in!

Jenny: This chlorine's stingin ma eyes. I'm gettin out.

Glen: Can I come and rub ye doon?

Jenny: Piss off! I'm goin in the sauna.

Basting

Liz: Is this no braw? I'm sweatin away here, it must be dead good for you. Is that no right, Dave?

Dave: Ye're damn right there. Course, when ye're as fit as I am, ye just kind of glow healthily in here. You dinnae look unfit yerself.

Liz: (*preening herself*) Aye, well I think it's awfy important, this exercise business.

Glen: I could go for this sauna bit regularly and forget about the exercise. I'm working up a brilliant thirst for the pub.

Jenny: I think I'm goin to die in here, it's that hot. I cannae breathe right. Why did I no just sit at home and stick my head in the oven? Are ye sure this is good for you?

Dave: Look, girls usually have a good time wi me an Glen no matter what we're doing. Could ye no relax a bit?

Liz: Aye, come on Jenny. She's no used to it, that's what it must be.

Glen: She's havin a good time, ay no hen?

He cuddles up to her.

Jenny: Get off!

Glen: Oh, ye're a wee bit sweaty are ye no? Am I that exciting?

Jenny: Bugger off!

Dave: Do youz two fancy comin to the pub efter this?

Jenny: No way!

Liz: Should we no go on the sunbeds first? I'm a bit pale.

Glen: Are ye no done through yet? Ye're no a piece o meat, ye ken!

Jenny: I bloody feel like one.

Dave: Stop whingin, you. Are youz wantin to come to the pub or no? I think it'd be a laugh, masel.

Liz: Aye, course we are.

Glen: Braw!

Jenny: Hmph.

Mutton

Dave: Hell's teeth! Did ye get a look at her in the corridor?

Glen: Aye, cannie be more than a day over fifty, and tarted up to the nines. Would ye no be embarrassed if yer mother came here lookin like that?

Liz: Aye, that one was along at the aerobics, wi her fat arse hingin oot they tracksuit bottoms she had on...

Jenny: Stop it! She's probably here cos she wants to be fit rather than mindin too much about the way she looks.

Glen: Well, she's lookin a bit better than you are! Ye're a wee bit flabby for somebody who comes here every week, are ye no?

Jenny: I don't usually come when Liz does, and I dinnae think I'll be back if the place is full of prats like you.

Liz: Come on, Jenny. He's just teasin.

Dave: I'm afraid my pal's just like that. You think with your dick, eh Glen!

Glen: That's what they say, and I can't say I've had many complaints! I know youz think this is a sauna, but ye're all actually sweatin cos youz are so close to my sexy body!

Dave: What, even me, Glen?

Glen: Especially you!

Cooking Times

Dave: That sauna was braw, but I think this steam bath is better.

Liz: Aye. I can feel the sweat runnin right down ma cleavage.

Glen: (*sotto voce*) I wish I could!

Dave: Maybe it's about time we made a move. Ye shouldnae spend too long in these things. You get all wrinkly.

Glen: Och! No yet. I'm gettin used to it.

Dave: I thought you were desperate for a pint?

Glen: Desperate? No me, Dave. My mind has been on other things. What about you, gorgeous? You dinnae want to go yet, do ye? You want to stay with me for a while, I'll bet!

As he speaks he reaches out and grabs Jenny, forcing his mouth on to hers. She lashes out at him.

Jenny: Bugger off, would ye! I dunno who you think you are, but I'd like to say that I've got one arsehole and that's enough!

She storms out.

Glen: She tasted a bit underdone, I reckon!

Dave: You're gonnae get yerself belted one of these days.

Liz: Ach, she's aye been a bit of a prude.

Dave: No like yerself then?

Liz: Oh, no!

Glen: So I take it there'll just be the three o us at the pub? A bit more to go round, you could say!

Food Presentation

Liz: I hope you're happy. You nearly lost me this date.

Jenny: So much for the exercise! You're welcome to both of them.

Liz: Are ye no comin, like? I've got lipstick an all that if you're worried about no lookin your best.

Jenny: So I see. You look just like that wifie you were slaggin off in there. Are those earrings no a bit on the flashy side for the pub?

Liz: Awbody's wearin these. They're trendy. You're just no wi it.

Jenny: An am I no glad!

Liz: Shut yer face. Are you comin or no?

Jenny: No. I'll see you back at the flat.

Liz: Aye, maybe.

Red Meat Aromas

Dave: Can I borrow yer deodorant?

Glen: Aye, here ye go. Lucky I brought this aftershave, eh?

Dave: Did ye? Guiz some o that.

Glen: Naw! This is my passion juice!

Dave: Aw, come on! She fancies me, that Liz. You've blown it wi her pal. You might as well go home.

Glen: I didnae hear her say she wanted to go out wi just you. I was thinkin more along the lines of a threesome!

Dave: That's the first bright idea you've had this decade!

The Case for Vegetarianism

Liz is walking along the street by herself, much later. She meets Jenny, who has come out to look for her.

Jenny: What happened to you?

Liz: Bloody prats! They sat an got pissed, then they made passes at me. Hands all ower ma tits an legs!

Jenny: What did you expect? They were treating you like meat all evening. You were acting like a brainless chicken.

Liz: I was drinkin cider an black. I didnae hae much energy to fend them off. But I think they decided another drink would be more exciting, so I left when they went to the bar again.

Jenny: Cider and black? You hate cider.

Liz: Tell me aboot it! I was just trying to impress them. They might have looked alright on the outside, but I think their brains had expired. Ugh! I feel…

Jenny: Yes? Healthier? Happier? Slimmer?

Liz: No! I think I'm going to…

  She pukes.

Maggie Stephen

Stuart A Paterson

Storm

The harsh labour of crows, a waking swell
Of noise shaking the leaves and benches, claws
Treading blackly on trees almost uprooted
In the evening storm of squabble outside.

In the mad dance I see some evidence
For the trail of lights on Callander road
And shake my fist through the opened window,
A fist like a small leaf fallen from high

In a downpour, trailing the building wind
From its fingers. Gradually falling, falling.

Cave People

You made for me this bed of arms,
Scooped cool pools for me to bathe
My hot self in. A cave of bone walls
You bade me live in, a green fire
You boiled from blood to wash my
Hands of stars and suns. Now I fear to
Stand beneath the sky's height, measure
On my brows the arches of land.
All because you made me hollow,
Dug the earth from under my skin.

Prelude

What hurt me most
Wasn't the flame
That trembled by candle
The edge of your eye.

It wasn't the ribbon
Preventing your hair
From rippling and hiding
The window and walls.

Nor was it the ember
That filled the ashtray,
The wine escaping
The stain of your lips.

What hurt me most
Were your fingers, splayed
Between us, long
And knuckle-white

Where they gripped and
Balled the rug, apart,
Into a shapeless
Messy thing.

Second Skin

Your clicking fingers gathered a frail rope
From the hills, conjuring warmth back into
Wool, weaving unspoken worries through
The frame of my chest, let my thin shoulders
Harness a tapestry patterned with you.

A decade hangs between the man and boy
You strove to warm. I worry that I'll miss
Cold sometimes. The cuffs have begun to frizz,
Wisps occasionally sloughing to the floor.
I carry you as you carried me before,
Or slip into remnants of old lovers
Made by others whose hands were not so sure.

Now I walk the hills in winter sun
That sends no heat and wrap myself around
Old sitting-stones; let the softened armour
Shield my skin and stroke my neck, a blanket
Holding a language of hands together,
Straightening my back by the precipice
Of dark-water light. The lambs on the crest
Must yield their coats. Not me. I breathe the twine
Of ribbed bone. One bloody thorn and I fall
Untangled and cold to a grave of air.

A Rush of Memory by Polmaise

At eleven I kissed the neighbourhood sweetheart,
Twelve she was, a stoneless peach then, furless
And ripe from the bough. It was a slap
Of wet concentration and closed eyes, tongueless
In the innocence of elevenishness and in
The spidery lair of a bin cupboard during
A preparatory dare for the coming school day.

At fifteen I kissed my first girlfriend,
Seventeen she was, a hairy rootmonger of men
All tousled from unmade beds. It was a suck
With a pull like a vacuum-cleaner. Tongueless
No more she forced the safety of my lips,
Seemed like she wanted my tonsils for a souvenir,
Welding our mouths with glue. I gargled later.

At sixteen I kissed my first love
For a whole three months, she was blond and frail
The way that kewpies are. It was summer,
And once I lay on top of her, in a field, young,
Hard as a hill, the dog's head cocked, no longer
Hoovering flies. If we'd gone one day
Without seeing each other we'd have died.

At seventeen I kissed a date ON THE TIT!
Twenty-one she was, immensely-nippled, almost
(But not quite) able to feed me, suckling, snorting away.
Mouths were irrelevant as we freed them to grab at
The mysterious sculpting and folds of flesh.
I tried to kiss her goodnight one time, she laughed
And groped me. Kissing was never the same.

At twenty-two I kissed a girl, cold dry
Funeral of love at a bus-stop, our first kiss,
One of farewell from two kindred souls
Who never dared broach the borders of cloth
Yet held hands for comfort in a friendless world.
As I watched her go, my lips hung open to reveal
A tongue for talking. Kissing was learning to speak.

Not long ago, skinned of promises,
I kissed a girl near a ruined castle, shaded
By majesty of sequoia, drawn to cool stone,
Lapped by water, wing, the essential solitude of kisses.

Cocooned

Now we have loosed the morning
On ourselves, it bullies in
The opened window, hectic freshness
Scattering the cobwebs' threaded
Maps throughout our lair. We should
Raise the cicatrix of sheet which
Scabs the lovemaking, let the
Voyeuristic trees breeze blushing
Curtains through festoons of lazy

Moving human skin and odour.
Instead I think once more we'll
Weave hard another carapace
Below the morning loosed to catch
A slow and naked languor
Struggling to recreate its absence.

An Old Monarch Visits the Peasants

Muddied boots in a corner. Half-emptied
Glass of malt by odd feet. A trail of grass
Front door to kitchen cupboard. Anxious cats
A blur round green-streaked trouser-bottoms
Opposite. A warmed hand rises slow to start
A voice long rusted to low. Untying my gaze,
You begin.
              At Whithorn recently, a friend
Tells me, there was unearthed a clarsach,
Whole, its finery preserved in peat. So they took
It to be cleaned, restored, found in Caithness
A lover of music with such an ear
For the old airs, such trust to his fingers.
The clarsach sung a treasure of tales
In a windless, fireless University room,
Nestled in a warm lap, singing through those
Hearing hands which held it.
                              Watching those lips
Moist with hospitality tune the dry
Air to readiness, my heart a clumsy bodhran
To the spring-clear constant ring of words,
Light shifts itself aside now to admit you.
Ears welcoming a cracked purity,
I settle back and listen to the land.

Stuart A Paterson

George Smith

The Yard

Every Sunday night, she was smaller;
rarely noticeable, but I knew;
knew that they had burned her, cut her,
ripped a little more of her life away;
and though I didn't know her name,
had never seen her lines unbroken,
I grieved.

She dwindled through the Summer, bloodlessly,
until one October evening,
the wharf leered emptily back at the moon.

They say that the Yard is no disgrace,
that all good ships must find their way there.
I no longer go that way.

The Great Divide

He was eight, and aggressive.
He said Are you a Catholic?
I wasn't sure.
He asked me what school I went to,
and I told him.
You're a Protestant, he told me,
so you're o.k.
My mouth said o.
Twenty-five years later, I'm no wiser.
I wonder if he is?

Glen Lyon Morning

Light thickened, and the river took on shape,
Coalescing from occasional teeth to a broken, grey field;
A body to the endless monologue
That underpinned the night-long conversation
Between rain and tent and petulant wind.

Still the light grew, inviting more sound,
And a blackbird eased delicate liquidity into the song.

Nothing more, until:
The flat, jangling discord of flung tent-pegs, the gasp
Of canvas on canvas, the muffled grunt of mild exertion,
And the soft, fading tramp of boots, Rannoch-bound.
The bent grass uncramped itself, slowly, cautiously.
The blackbird, in silence, laid his ambush.

Moondancer

Stepping flickering ghostly across the screen,
his deep-fried voice proclaimed history
into the early-morning living room,
where a sleep-starved ten-year-old sat,
desperately trying to feel historical at this,
the greatest moment since the creation.

I failed, then, to feel appropriate wonder,
distracted by the snuffling sleep
of the black-and-tan hound whose muzzle
breathed earth-bound dreams onto my legs.
Besides, his proclamation was lost to me
in the hissing hostile void between us.

But as I was carried to bed in indulgent arms,
he danced again for me, slow-motion,
lightly spurning worlds with unbound feet,
the first of an armoured, faceless pantheon.

The dance is in my blood now,
and my dreams might have been his.

Damned Rain

Rain came, riven from the slate sky,
stippling the faces of the puddles in the yard
with countless loving caresses.
And as I watched, through dirty windows and bars,
I remembered times across the sea of years
when I had cursed the rain, railed at the sky,
and wished myself indoors.

.Then, as I stood there in pain, I wondered
what price I would pay to be loved by the rain,
as the dim, weary grey yard was loved;
and my heart filled with the ache of knowing
that however low a price was asked,
I could not pay.

Buskers

The Saturday sun sang golden
on the restless trombone slide,
licked lasciviously at the clarinet keys,
and cut a rug with the banjo's strings.

They made it into a contest
between themselves and the haughty organ
that bludgeoned the air through open church doors,
moaning through strictured praises
to its tone-deaf god.

And the gathering crowd gave the verdict:
the song in the cool was subdued
by the cool on the Green.

George Smith

Ad-man's Dream

Elspeth Stewart

Clifford Johnston is very successful in television advertising. Surprising really for he is a bumbling idiot at home.

"You are a bumbling idiot", his wife exclaims fondly as the mower runs away with him, damaging his perfect suburban Edinburgh garden.

"Sorry Marty", he smiles contritely, his craggy masculine face taking on the penitent bulldog expression his wife so loves.

Marty soon sorts everything out. A bird of freedom, she swoops from the freezer to microwave and soon she and Clifford are chatting amicably round the perfectly set table with baby gurgling on the floor licking a hygienic lollipop he has picked up from the germ free floor.

There is a brief disturbance as the younger children join them, a boy, James and a girl, Emma.

"FEED ME", they demand as they rush to the table but they are at the cutie-pie age and of course Marty and Clifford smile indulgently for Marty has foreseen their needs. She had filled the cooker with oven-chips and with a bowl of these in front of them James and Emma are content.

Meanwhile poor old Clifford who has managed to drive his new BMW from the Outer Hebrides in time for a pre-dinner Martini dry enough for a macho man, can't find his mouth and drops beetroot down the front of his best shirt. Contrite bumbling look again. Chorus of "Oh Dad", from the children, and teenage son Garth who has rushed in, desperate to wash his shirt before dashing out again. Of course he doesn't know which machine is the washing machine and tries to clean it in the microwave with the wrong brand of washing powder. (Marty has a cupboard full of wrong brands just to teach her family a lesson.)

Marty rises, still smiling, in her bright white tracksuit – no chewing-gum-white here – taking everything in her stride with simplicity. Throwing away the ordinary washing powder she accepts some doubtfully from a handsome stranger much less bumbling than Clifford.

"I have just had this stuff tested and it beat the leading brand." He smiles a deprecating smile.

"How clever", breathes Marty hoping that the handsome stranger will lurk about in the perfect garden, finishing the mowing and puffing cigars. He is the sort of man (not the married sort) who can turn a crisis into another chance of getting lung cancer in the most disarming way.

Marty remembers to rinse the shirts with a leading softener. Emma, aged eight is testing them for softness and Susie, the little girl from next door has gone home crying, her mother got her washing all wrong again by using the other leading brand.

"Susie probably hasn't had her Mars-a-day or even a finger of fudge", remarks Marty.

James, aged ten, has to change the baby's nappy which was leaking because Daddy had bought the wrong sort. James finds Garth with a bucket over his head in the bathroom and douses him with anti-spot cream wishing that Garth had a twin to use as a control. Just as well he doesn't though, for the Johnson family are already out of line with more than two-point-something children.

Dad, back from admiring the car has got himself caught in the playpen. Marty is ironing the two shirts and sniffing thoughtfully and reminiscing about the last time they were worn. Baby Pete is toddling about demonstrating the effectiveness of his nappy. Baby is of course more sensible than Dad and of course Garth, who is maturing into bumbling-idiot-the-second.

"This is how it should be," reflects Dad, "this is how men are." Except men who smoke cigars or wear Levis or drink a lot of Coke, or have just bought a car.

Marty is beginning to wonder if she can get out in time to meet the man in the garden when in walks Mother-in-Law.

"I don't like those new-fangled irons", she croaks. She is fat and annoying though sometimes she can be the salt of the earth. Swiftly Marty demonstrates that she can do everything better than anyone else, especially old fashioned Mother-in-Law. She is now ready to escape even the demands of her blond curly daughter and football-playing son.

"Must go for a driving lesson", she lies. She is good at lying or at least economical with the truth for she conceals the nature of most of the meals, it being apparently necessary for Clifford to believe that she spends all day preparing them.

Clifford comes back from the garage to find his Mother-in-Law clearing up the cat-sick. She has apparently given Tiddles the wrong brand.

Marty smiles patronisingly as Mum pours him, (Clifford, not the cat) a bowl of cornflakes. "Cornflakes, I ask you?" she thinks, having been converted to new-fangled muesli. But she ponders that the world is returning to old values like pure natural butter or almost butter and clear natural shampoos and natural bread and almost natural washing powder if non-biological means natural which sounds odd if you think about it but of course Marty doesn't. Maybe cornflakes have a good old-fashioned nostalgia appeal.

Dad eats his cornflakes thoughtfully managing not to spill anything down his shirt-front, to everyone's disappointment. The truth is he is worried and does not want to bring the man with the newly-tested washing powder in again. How can this man worry him in the best of all possible advertising man's dream families?

"There's a strange smell around here" is all he says, and for the first time is irritated by Marty's clever use of the latest, most publicised air-freshener.

"Tobacco or dog smells?" she enquires sweetly, spreading a biscuit for mother.

illustration by Alan Chapman, Printmaker's Workshop

"Edamie", she explains with the superior tolerance she extends to all the family as if dealing with pigmies on a visit to Harrods.

"Tobacco – cigars", he mutters darkly. Clifford wonders whether a treat would relax him, a Kit-Kat perhaps. A leading brand of cola would of course put everything right. Everyone knows that happiness, friendship, love and personal beauty result from drinking the right cola.

"No cola?" He asks.

"They were out of it." Marty lies having been learning karate instead of shopping.

"Bad distribution", mutters Clifford taking a leading bar of chocolate from his pocket. He turns his back on the family while he eats it. Yes, he is dreaming. He is away on a beach, but something is wrong with this dream. He is advancing on the washing-powder man with an axe. He is...

"Are you ill dear?" Marty is shaking his shoulder gently. "It must be a cough." She spoons a foul-tasting liquid into his mouth. Surely that can't be one of the leading brands of cough – Arghh.

"But it was all so perfect", he gasps.

The last thing he sees is the open 'fridge with row upon row of convenience meals. As he writhes on the ground he hears the insistent chant of "FEED ME FEED ME FEED ME" fading. His mother looks old and sad. Her bones are swollen with arthritis. His children are indifferently munching chocolate that rots their teeth but leave their hands without stain. His wife is standing by him with a mop and bucket to clean up around him.

This can't be the real world. Surely everything would come right if only they all sat down for a cup of tea. But it is going dark.

"Lighting", he mutters. "Badly lit set. Wrong argh light. Looking at it in the wrong light."

A man steps in from the garden, He takes in the body by the coal-glow fire, the wife pouring the rest of the essence of deadly nightshade, (a completely natural substance), down the sink, a despised mother-in-law having a stroke unnoticed, a washing machine pouring soapy water over the floor, the burning odour of sweaty clothes, a baby dabbling in a pool, of cat-sick, a young man emerging from the bathroom with green hair, either for ecological reasons or because it matches his dinner, and a ten-year-old boy having a breakdown.

"Should I call the police, the fire brigade, the hospital?" he enquires with macho calm.

"Fuck off", screams Marty.

He smiles the smile of a man who has it all sussed, who always knew it was all a dream. He walks into the sunlight of the garden, and, turning his back on the mayhem, he lights a small cigar. Resignedly he coughs a little natural blood into his whiter-than-white handkerchief.

Elspeth Stewart

Mairi NicGumaraid

Soraidh Leibh

Soraidh leibh
Nuair a thig oirbh
A dhol a Cheann Trá a sheasamh
Ris An t-Amhran Náisiúnta
'S a dh'aideachadh
Gu na dh'fhàg sibh a' Bhàn-righ aig an taigh

A bheil amhran agaibhs'
Dh'fhaighnich fear an taighe
Tha
Chan eil
Tha
Dè fear?
Flower of Scotland
O chan e
Nach e?
Dè eile?
'Soraidh leibh
Is oidhche mhath leibh'
Is mise còmh' ribh
Le beag nàire
Na mo laige leis a' ghàire

Cha b' e sin a bha iad ag iarraidh
An Ceann Trá an Contae Chiarrai
Ach 's e fhuair iad
'S sheas iad ris
Cho modhail balbh
Is rinn sinne falbh
Mar fhògarraich

Is iadsan 'Laochra Fáil
Atá faoi gheall ag Eirinn'

Is sinne sluagh na dàil
A tha ro mhall ag èirigh

Ach thog sinn Flùr na h-Alb' an Tamhlacht
Agus leag sinn an taigh

Mary Montgomery

Fare Thee Well

Fare thee well
When you have to
Go to Ventry to stand
To A Soldier's Song
And admit
You left the Queen at home

Do you have an anthem
Asked the host
Yes
No
Yes
Which one?
Flower of Scotland
Oh no
No?
What else?
Soraidh Leibh
And goodnight
And me with you
Unashamedly
Weak laughing
That wasn't what they wanted

In Ventry in County Kerry
But that is what they got
And they stood to it
Polite and quiet
And we left
Like refugees

Soldiers are they
'Whose lives are pledged to Ireland'

We are the people of delay
Who are too slow to rise

But we raised the Flower of Scotland in Tallaght
And brought the house down

Rud a Dh'innsinn Dha M' Athair

Nis tha 'n t-iasg air ais anns a' Choille 'bhainn
'S dòch' am breac 's am bradan òg
'S tha an eala bhàn 's na tunnagan
Air tilleadh dhan chanàl

Nam biodh e fhathast beò

Tha gealbhoinn tighinn nan coithional
Gu taobh thall na sràid
Is dà chalman a' fuireach fon uinneig
Mar gum b' ann leotha bha 'n àit

Tha mi ga ionndrainn fhathast

Tha fear às an Eilean Sgitheanach
A' fuireach ri mo thaobh
An diugh air a dhreuchd a leigeil dheth
Ach chleachd e bhith na shaor

Chòrdadh e ris dhol a chèilidh air

Tha tè de chàirdean mo mhàthar
Ag obair faisg air làimh
'S tè de mhuinntir Bhail'Ailein
As a' bhùth ud thall

Bhiodh fhios aige cò iad

Tha iasg ùr ri cheannach
Aig a' bhan ud shuas
'S buntàta tighinn o thaobh Inbhir Air
'S bainn' a' bhotail steach on tuath

Bhithinn dachaigheil ris

What I would tell my father

The fish are back in the Kelvin
Trout, perhaps, and young salmon
And the white swan and the ducks
Have returned to the canal

If he were still alive

The sparrows congregate
Across the street
And two pigeons live below my window
As if they owned the place

I still miss him

A man from Skye
Lives next door
He's now retired
He used to be a joiner

He would enjoy visiting him

A cousin of my mother's
Works close by
And a girl from Balallan
Works in that shop

He would know who they are

There's fresh fish for sale
At the van up there
And Ayrshire potatoes
And bottled milk from the farm

I'd make him feel at home

Robin Jenkins

Homemaker

A thousand miles from home, moonlight sparkles
On these white houses, but it is our own
I see in my mind, white too, on the hill
Above the Firth, sad and lonely. Among
The rhododendrons sheep and their lambs
Shelter. They think the house is deserted.
But it is not empty. You are present.
You come often but only when nobody's there.
That is the condition we must accept.
You go forward eagerly, as you always did.
No one ever loved life more than you.
The house is familiar and yet strange.
You have brought with you other intimations.
Here is your Christmas cactus, in flower again.
It is being well looked after. You smile.
Down on the shore a curlew calls, in a field
A cow complains, an owl cries in the wood:
Melancholy sounds. You listen bravely.
In our room you notice changes: your bed
Removed, your wardrobe gone, your clothes given away.
You approve. We must get on with our lives.
But there are tears in your eyes. I had thought
Only the living knew sorrow and pain.
Beloved homemaker, you pass from room
To room, restoring the magic that you gave
To every household thing.

Tavira

One morning we went by bus to Tavira.
A riverside town twelve miles east of Faro.
The sun shone, but as always it was you
Who transfigured everything, even the stray
Cantankerous dogs. Did you know
That was how I felt? Did you see
It in my eyes, hear it in my voice?
No, it was a secret I kept too jealously.

To most visitors Tavira is a fair
Little town with its pleasant river,
Its white churches and green gardens,
But I remember it as a place where

You stand smiling at me, though forever
Out of my reach, like Eurydice.
There are so many such places now,
Like Kabul and Kota Kinabalu,
Unlikely heavens; but in Tavira
By the river, with the sun shining on your brow
And your hair enhaloed,
You look so eager.

Waiting

Here she would wait for me, on this mound
Golden with whins, in the field of sheep.
She would see the ferry, funnels red
As rowanberries, sailing staunchly
In and out of Rothesay Bay; a submarine,
Black as a beetle, sneaking out to sea
With its cargo of uncountable deaths;
Yachts white-winged like butterflies;
And towering over all the Sleeping Warrior.
"If you want to go on I'll wait here."
And sometimes, eager for wider views
I would go on, until high in the heather,
I could see, in the Sound between
Arran and Bute, Inchmarnock,
Island of ancient graves. Soon I would hurry back
And we would go home together, down
The avenue of misshapen beeches,
Listening to birdsong and looking out for deer.

She is not here today, or any day.
As if I was a child I am assured
That she is waiting for me in heaven.
Her body, like Christ's, was resurrected.
But what I saw was dust blown in the wind.
Like a child I ask guileless questions.
Where is heaven? Do all dead people go there,
Even the black children who die of hunger?
Is there room for so many? Do not some
Go to hell where they suffer forever?
And like a child I am answered with evasions,
Fairytales, myths, and hopeful lies.

It is a matter of faith, they admit in the end:
Believing what you want or need to believe.
What they really mean is they do not know.
Neither do I, but since the evidence

Is all against it I cannot convince myself
That May, restored and happy, waits
In some divine dispensation where whins
Lack thorns and there is no sorrow or pain
Or loss or grief or disappointment.

I wait here, in tears, remembering her.
That is all I have or ever can have.

Desolation

It is three a.m. The gale howls and rain
Batters against the windows. Racked by pain
I wait till the pain-killer takes effect,
Alone, sorry for myself. I recollect
That Tristan Shandy's father, amusing man,
Was afflicted by sciatica too and
Had to endure it without co-drymenol.
I smile a little and then I recall
How once, suffering pain worse than this, you wept
And I could do nothing to help except
Weep with you. You were not able to appreciate
My useless tears. I do not now wait
For these stounds in my leg to be suppressed.
They are nothing. It is your distressed
Memory I want to comfort and placate.
Forgive me. I have never felt so desolate.
I still cannot believe that you are dead.
So many necessary things remained unsaid
Even after our marriage of fifty years.
I say some of them now but no one hears.
Outside the storm grows in fury. By dawn
Leaves, flowers, twigs and slates will litter the lawn.
After a while I take my stick and creep
Back to our bedroom. I shall try to sleep.

Next Morning

After the storm quietness
Prevails. In the meadows
Sheep graze, obliviously.
Two, foot-rotted, are kneeling.
Others limp painfully.
They have forgotten the fierce darkness,
The huddle in the copses,
The soaked fleeces,
And the crash of breaking branches.

Perhaps one or two did not survive.
Do not call them mindless creatures.
They are a comfort to me this morning.
They help put right the pieces
So badly out of order
Last night. Ewe calls anxiously
To lamb and lamb replies.
I listen gratefully.
I am asked to remember
That she I mourn was far more often
Happy than plaintive, and that
For us all there must be an ending.

On the Firth the Rothesay ferry
Sails round Toward Point, its passengers
Relieved at so safe a journey
After last night's tempest.
Some may look up and wonder
Who lives in the lonely cottage
On the hill. He has their blessing,
Whoever he is, and they have mine.

Robin Jenkins

SACRED
STONES
SACRED
PLACES

by Marianna Lines

with photography by
Paul Turner

*'Stones can tell many stories, and con-
tain a great history which pervades every
crack and cranny of their makeup. While
every stone in the world is important in
its own particular role, certain stones
have been made* SACRED *by the messages
written upon them, etched into their
surface by the hands of ancient peoples,
and by their association with the
spiritual history of Scotland ....'*

A lovingly documented exploration of
some very remarkable monuments to
Scotland's intriguing heritage. The
author, a well-known artist, comple-
ments photographic images with
beautiful and intricate impressions of
stone-art delicately taken from original
sources.

Cased/0 7512 0652 4/176pp/£19.95

SAINT ANDREW PRESS
121 George Street, Edinburgh EH2 4YN

Gavin Bowd

Mining

*White the land of snow
And white the backs
Striped with bone.*

*To cut this shaft to Africa
Until the stone wears red embers,
And the blood pumps, the skin steams
In the fiery dance.*

*So cold this vault of invisible stone.
Wait:*

*The jewels will appear like stars
Who love to hide.*

*– They will never be ours.
Cantos rising to their starry vault,
The monks,
Our owners,
The promising wise:*

*"So much love when your body takes
The worm."*

Yards away behind the rock,
Hear them:

Roots are binding their net of strength.

No sleep from the nourishing noise.

Six days of hunger rock
Then Sunday,

Coloured cloak of the arrowed glass,
Black stones for the begging child,

Hours of fire to lick the hands
To work again.

Lifting the pick

Then dropping it,
Cracking the rock
Then splitting it.

Illustration by Joanne E Grant

Dragging the coal to the Methil sun
And hating it.

Mining,
Losing,
Remembering
The golden promise by the harbour wall,
The land of diamond dream.

Eyes were straining beneath the light,
The full-blooded light,
The sea light
That beat the breath

From the chest where the flood of hair,
The milk root hair,
The good hair
Guarded panting warmth.

When the moon is gathering the planet's clouds
In hurricane hands,
And the giant is rising to the thousand sky,
The waves of tar,

It's good to follow
The leafy crevice
To the warm, round breast of the nesting bird
Then leave.

Cold gentleness,
Hunger heart,
Mine of respect.

Many more bodies will be sealed in rock
For the pyramids of slag,
Many more hearths to cover in spit
For mining.

Then around the tower
The stranger of silence.

The long-sealed wound of the winding-shaft
Is calling him,
The boy who never left the stone's
Magnificence,

To plunge the magma's
Black catastrophe,
To touch the spangled root,

At dawn to free the flesh
Warm from lawful eating.

Summertime

The pregnant woman waited by the door,
Breathing air from the heavy sheaves.
So much goodness was ripening
In the frenzied flesh of the pear.

And so much strength in the whirlwind
Of the oakwood carved as a door,
In the grey engraving of the mere,
Abandoned the struggle then slept.

On the crackling flame of the twigs,
The little girl already fixed
Her eyes of agate for tomorrow,

At the foot of the bed, where the dead
Lay under white sheets rotting,
While the hawk never questioned their fate.

Clearing

At the extreme limit, the trunks
Offer silver against the depths,
And the dead, spread wide and crystalline,
Lose moss to the sucking roots.

Today or tomorrow, the spoors
Wait for following legs,
Ears listening after the branches,
Fainting eyes and trembling holly.

Red earth without our souls.
Bird conversations in mists.
Bark patterns on my life-lines.

In this clearing, at the extreme limit,
Not even the wind's play of fir
Drowns the wailing of the saws.

CCCP

Astride the balcony, Marina applauds
Another frigid goodbye of a harvest moon.
For a thousand miles her image arrives
Of fire scattering upon the land.

The frontiers are safe, we read, the gates
Of our city shelter snoring guards,
And through the alleyways lolling dogs chase
Another red sunrise on the red planet.

The leaves are burning, the grapes fermenting,
The child unfurling in your distant quilt,
This fall, Marina, when your worry insists:

Your son expelled in the invisible town,
The rout of shade in the teeming noon,
Your union torn in blood and urine.

Religio

The line that binds to the hidden fields,
The expanse of ocean, its air
That the gull strains its arms to beat.
The line that binds to the trees,
Breaking on the bud, shooting
Chaos into the beautiful.

The line that binds which is hidden,
Which threatens to tear on this
Broken glass of the vision city,
The array of chimneys, pipes and walls
Which have captured daylight and will not
Tell us where it is hidden.

The line that blinds which is traced
By us blind to the promised order
And treading on debris of myths and gods,
Stretching up for the muthos mouth,
The kiss of moss on stone,
High in the frost where gentian strikes.

Decades

Snow lay before us, the newly arrived,
Set in an air that drew our voices,
Left the branches' web of down
– A storm had fallen to astonish.

Clouds muffled the lights of the town
And cars crawled home in columns,
Old men relinquished the libraries,
Mothers emptied fields of glitter.

Here, the treetops held the last apples
And athletes ran the valley's curve
As I felt our decades subside:

Your tender crush upon the bark,
Our feet dug quivering in the path,
My forehead nuzzled in your bleeding mouth.

Zoo

Your crown of black feathers won't help you
To dissolve these bars for dominion,
And that tail of silky rope
Is wanting the bush's spell.

And those paws pushed to catch the sun
Won't mix the leaves with your spots
And the spitting roar and yellow eyes
Are made for the laugh of a child.

Swept by clippers and cotton fields,
You were brought to this bare floor
Where a gaze blasts the mountain of dream:

Jason braced in ebony bronze
Sinking the necks of cringing bulls
Whose collars catch electric lights.

Gavin Bowd

John Dixon

The Halt at Ballinluig

The train had stopped there like a parting
on the hillside. Ten o'clock. He looked
his watch up. It was lighter than the night
had been all summer, mystifyingly
so, almost sad, with something of the past
about it, but not only that. What was
it then? For half an hour he felt his life-
time out along the silence, trying not
to listen at it for an answer to
himself but lying all the same until
the dusk collected his belonging there
up in the dark and he remembered what
it must have been like once, or might have been
when everything meant what he said, and did,
if only in that dream he kept on having.
Even now it almost happened, but
not quite. Instead he stared a moment at
this stream that he would never see again
and heard the train grind to a start on up
the line. It wasn't worth remembering.

Dumbarton Castle

And so it goes,
The grass has grown another afternoon.
Half the light looks as if it could
Have been begun for dawn
But that's not quite what the dusk has in mind
Or the lamps that have come on
In the station.
Soon the whole town will turn
Into a train with nowhere to go
But tomorrow
And the day after that.
It's got so that the council estate
Is already a television
And the half-closed countryside unthought of;
Lost it would look like the coast
Of another land or astronomer's miscalculation
Ten light centuries
From the time that's on now.
And so on down to the crummiest cafe
And most complete absence of everything
Since someone was on their way home;
And all to make space
For a castle that'll becalm
In the same moat
As "Mitzi's Continental Cosmetics Shop."
And why not? Most of the portcullis
Could have become a "Keep Left" sign
And might still,
It's only a matter of time.
Once I dreamed Mediæval leaves
On the trees and looked
To the east window for a handkerchief –
Or something.
All that happened was me though
And that wasn't enough.
It isn't now
And will never be,
However much I shade my light in
Or imagine it doesn't mean anything.
Only the dark'll make sense of us,
Just as it does to a television screen
That's been turned on and off
So many times it could be
The view from a night train window
Onto eternity.

Easter at Blenheim

An oak-panelled park sprinkled with copses,
Backs of crypts scrubbing the brass, marble,
Busts and ornaments; alabaster trees.
        Why lease the past
        Aliases
Whatever air's asbestosing the prayers
Of this sparse April parlour must splutter
To dust until it dismantles itself.
        And ash fire? Dreams
        Are dismembered
It doesn't matter whether threats of death
Dripping splash us sepulchres, scrap
Basilisks or spectres. April parts us.
        In all eras,
        Love frays and dies.
Authors, thrones and history know Jester's praise
Whoever is emperor now and stay
Until they are traded for a better laugh.
        The scent which we
        Imprison is
Surprising? Not to purists, no: this pin-
Table light will be here tomorrow and
The day after, there's no other fabric.
        The sad perfume
        Of a ghost. Why?
The wind coils rattlesnake hard in the tired
Hills and slows; although it is not autumn
Or winter something, somewhere, is dying.

Virgo

"The stars are unadulterated trash",
she said, as if to put their horoscope
away. "They don't expect to end in ash,
but that's what happens, and besides, they slope
off home when everything is over. What
on earth's the point of that, apart from some
more light, those little whiles that haven't got
tomorrow, just their yesterdays to come
and go with. No, you might as well re-floor
the whole live show right now; although" – and here
she touched the night along its landing – "I
could take off further if it wasn't for
this world of mine. To where things just appear
to be, and are; to never saying die."

Illustration by Fiona M Girvan

The Two Of Me

A shadow passed, it passed me by,
it passed towards the day I'll die.
No empty mention of my name
impassioned dust or stupid shame
no muffled love or failed desire
was ever so afraid of fire.

I looked along a lane and saw
the shadow there deployed once more.
The cold had locked it into place
and darkness kept it back a space.
"Remember me", it seemed to say.
"I'll open up another day".

So down I went, the way I'd climbed
out-talking what my dreams had mimed,
until I lost the stairs out loud,
and looked to see their darkness crowd
into another-worldly light
that led my shadow down the night.

Three Party Pieces

1

Speech slammed some more
It mimicked the dark
Took a chord out of the piano
And strangled everything;
No one said what they meant
Just toured each other with words.
And at the end of all that?
There was nothing.
The north side of a "desert air".

2

"Well did you or didn't you?"
He soaked his words in her
And listened – "I don't care to say."
That's where their time went,
The light's too. Half-an-hour
Felt like a snapshot, the crash
Of photography striving for after.
It might not have happened, but did.
"I was a star".

3

Masks were coming off
And put back on as cowls;
A black cardboard box
Kept them absorbed –
Big packets of drink there –
"Tequila Darling?"
That and the lank air
The hanging gardens of dark.
It would soon be outside.
Everywhere.

John Dixon

SCOTTISH
Affairs

The new quarterly Journal. Its purpose is to encourage research and debate on topics that are of particular interest in Scotland. It is independent of all political parties and pressure groups.

Issue number 2
(January 1993)

* Local initiatives in economic and social development

* The EC summit

* Gender and Scottish identity

Annual subscriptions (4 issues) £20.00

Unit for the Study of Government in Scotland
31 Buccleuch Place
Edinburgh
EH8 9JT

Reviews

Cultural Weapons

Scotland's Music, John Purser, Mainstream, £25; *Tree of Strings*, Keith Sanger & Alison Kinnaird, Kinmor Music, £19.95/£14.95; *Scottish Art 1460–1990*, Duncan Macmillan, Mainstream, £45

It is a shame, in a way, that such a monumental landmark of Scottish cultural history as BBC Radio Scotland's epic documentary series *Scotland's Music* was given to such an ephemeral medium as radio; and it is a triumph for Mainstream to have rendered the landmark tangible in John Purser's *Scotland's Music*. It is a magnificent work in both its breadth and depth of scholarship: excellently presented, furnished with countless musical examples, written with clarity and passion in equal measure.

The words 'clarity' and 'passion' might be taken as slogans for the two divergent forces that run through all musical history: on the one hand the elegance, refinement and intellect of 'art' music, on the other untutored, instinctive, Dionysiac 'folk' music. For me, foremost among the achievements of *Scotland's Music* is the way it shows both fabrics to be woven from a common thread, that thread being spun from a variety of numinous perceptions not exclusively Christian.

The role of the bard, and therefore of poetry, is given careful attention in discussing the roots of Scottish music. There is a kind of tidal symbiosis between Irish musical archaeology and the Scots Gaelic oral tradition that lends strength to each other. Certainly the traffic between the two peoples was a vital force, and once Columban Christianity developed in the north-west, the Celtic fondness for patterns found its way into the chanting of the monks. Purser traces that link through to Carver, and on to modern-day Gaelic psalmody.

Purser shows that, for Gaeldom, music was, and remains, the sword of the language, the most effective defence against cultural invasion from the south.

In the period between the reformation and the present day, in terms of 'art' music at least,

I find it difficult to share Purser's enthusiasm. With the Court moving to London and Scots noblemen taking elocution lessons, arguably the patrons of the arts lost their ear for Scotland at this point. It is a thorny area, because on the one hand there are excellent cultural reasons for researching with all diligence; on the other hand the music simply isn't very good. That would be occasion for regret were it not for the fact that Scotland is enjoying its musical Golden Age right now through the intellect and passion of such younger composers, justly celebrated in the closing chapter, as Judith Weir, James Dillon and James MacMillan (to name only the most outstanding).

I enjoyed fighting line by line through certain passages of *Scotland's Music*. Occasionally Purser takes on the persona of *Absolutely*'s 'McGlashan', averring 'Scots invented that' right left and centre. For the most part, I might add, Purser convinces me – I find it hard to swallow the notion that Monteverdi's use of the harp in *Orfeo* was influenced by the Gaelic clarsach, but it's not so unreasonable. That the idea of bowing stringed instruments came from the Middle East in the wake of the Crusades, on the other hand, doesn't (to my recollection) tally with accounts of the Crwth I read as a student.

Scotland's Music represents a point in time, a point where it is – just – possible to squeeze an entire history of the nation's music into one book. Secondmost of its achievements is to stand as a giant fingerpost pointing the way towards many fascinating avenues of research. The future awaits!

Tree of Strings (*Crann nan Teud*) represents exactly that kind of work. Subtitled 'a history of the harp in Scotland', it follows the development of the instrument from 8th century Pictish rock carvings through its decline by the 16th/17th centuries, to its modern revival.

For a work of scholarship, it is not necessarily a compliment to say that the book is at its most enjoyable when thigh-deep in the semi-magical mists of Celtic Christianity. Pulling together so many different legends has its own validity, nevertheless, if some discipline and analysis is applied to them.

I don't mean to imply that *Crann nan Teud* is entirely a collection of legends: there is a great deal of painstaking documentation of information not hitherto published, which makes the book a highly valuable reference. A tendency to flit back and forth from place to place, to overwhelm with names, dates and places, mars it unfortunately; also more musical examples would have been useful. These defects all point to a small production budget, which goes a long way towards excusing them while demanding that such projects should be more generously provided for in future.

Duncan Macmillan's *Scottish Art 1460–1990* is sib to *Scotland's Music*: for all that it is a very different book, as the subject dictates. Where music embraces the whole cultural spectrum, fine art doesn't – the equivalent to folk music in contemporary art terms might be said to be graffiti. Alternatively photography, which of course is a whole subject on its own.

The question arises whether this relative narrowness comes from the author or the subject. Macmillan doesn't write with the passion of Purser: *Scottish Art* doesn't share *Scotland's Music*'s crusading tenor. For all that, Macmillan is unquestionably thorough within his remit, and the result *is* glorious. Woven through with colour illustrations, *Scottish Art* presents a full and vivid account of its subject. The great artists – the Ramsays, the Wilkies, the Cadells or the Campbells – all leap off the page thanks to superb reproduction, and these are matched with a lucid and informative narrative which, like *Scotland's Music,* is written in direct, accessible language.

Although great detail is given on the work of the masters, care is taken to place them in their context. Allan Ramsay, son of the great poet, spent most of his working life based in London. Macmillan – it's hard to resist painterly similes – inks in the political, intellectual and cultural background to the period in Scotland before making a convincing reclamation of Ramsay's reputation as the greatest portrait painter of his era. It's akin to restoration, lifting the shadow Reynolds' reputation cast over him. Just as *Scotland's Music* makes the ephemeral permanent, so Macmillan here consolidates the impact made by the National Gallery's recent Ramsay exhibition.

In repeating this consolidation over the chapters Macmillan focusses attention on the immense cultural value of Scottish art, focussing attention too on that dusty, overtrodden road to London. Like *Scotland's Music, Scottish Art* is a rallying point: both are cultural weapons of the finest steel. Pick them up.

Peter Cudmore

Dunn Scotus, Alvarez Europae

The Faber Book Of Twentieth Century Scottish Poetry, ed Douglas Dunn; *The Faber Book Of Modern European Poetry*, ed A Alvarez, both Faber & Faber, £17.50

Douglas Dunn's task of trimming the Scottish poetry of this century to fit inside the covers of a single volume can't have been easy, no more than the parallel task of summarising it in the introductory essay 'Language and Liberty'. The disputes which publication have aroused in Scotland seem to suggest that 'the Faber book' of any kind of poetry is expected to meet a standard of discrimination more stringent than any other publisher, as if the ghost of T S Eliot continues to oversee the art from its spiritual home at 3 Queen Square, London. And it is with Eliot that Dunn begins: in fact, the whole volume might be viewed as a case for the defence of Scottish literature, accused by Eliot's 1919 assertion that "there is no longer any tenable distinction to be drawn for the present day between the two (English and Scottish) literatures."

This is Dunn's point of departure, from which he sets out to show that Eliot's prediction for the demise of Scottish literature was mistaken, with the consequence that the poems selected must display 'Scottishness', which he labels "a quality open to crass exaggeration as well as more subtle forms of garbled excess" in his introduction. Well and good, were it not for the lingering suspicion that the volume's 'Scottishness' seems once again to be defined in the negative, by how it differs from 'Englishness', as has been the case so often in the past. The suspicion that this is a volume which has to justify its existence to its own publishers lingers.

As might be expected, the space given over to MacDiarmid is large. For Dunn, he seems to be both reviver and reductionist in turn, the liberator of the right to write in Scots who directly challenged the attitude epitomised in the Eliot quotation, who then became the oppressor of less obviously rooted poetic spirits like W S Graham, whom Dunn rightfully places firmly in the Scottish tradition. Of the disagreement spurred by Edwin Muir's *Scott and Scotland*, Dunn writes that "MacDiarmid's counter-attack is usually regarded as having won the day"; then he follows this with a lengthy extract from Muir and a summation of the fairly dismal situation of the writer in Scotland at that time, which seems to find agreement with Muir's view of the linguistic void at the centre of Scots-based Scottish literature. This is preparatory to Dunn's optimism over the state of poetry in Scotland now: "between the three languages of Scotland, writers have managed to negotiate a climate of opinion which allows the freedom to write in the tongue in which a poet feels most at home"; an optimistic note which is a fair example of Dunn's overall tone, avoiding polemic in an attempt to show the rift of the earlier part of the century as healed.

It is the fate of all anthologies to be less than full and there are obvious criticisms to be made. The selection of poems and poets is open to dispute: personal favourites are absent and certain omissions such as Ian Hamilton Finlay or George Bruce appear glaring, though none more so than the editor's decision to omit himself; the treatment of the recent Kenneth White phenomenon seems cursory; the closing pages, roughly covering those poets born after 1950, are even-handed in terms of allocation of space compared with the earlier period, where estimation of the poet's importance appears to be illustrated by the number of pages the work fills. No doubt Dunn wishes to reserve judgement on these younger writers, which is understandable, yet could be read as if there have been no remarkable Scottish poets born since that time.

The approach of the end of the century will no doubt encourage further attempts on definitive twentieth century anthologies of various poetries in a decade's time. For the present, generally speaking, Douglas Dunn has performed a sterling service to the Scottish variety by this undertaking. I feel sure that the book is substantial enough in quantity and quality to convince Eliot's ghost of the project's worth.

In contrast, Al Alvarez is under no particular pressure to satisfy a localised readership in editing *The Faber Book of Modern European Poetry*. He confesses it to be a personal selection at the outset. Reading through it, the fact that the word 'modern' is trapped inside a particular historical period is underlined once more. This is not a book of 'happening' poetry. Alvarez makes certain concessions to the changing map of Europe with national listings which include Serbia and Russia, as opposed to Yugoslavia and the Soviet Union, but the task of keeping up with shifts in borders and names seems pointless anyway, as all the poets included emerged from the pre-1989 Europe.

This would have been a wonderful opportunity to gather the new work emerging from the "boiler-room" underground in the east together with the cutting edge of poetry in the west, to draw together the new Europe. Instead, we are offered more or less the familiar cast of known stars: Milosz, Holub, Celan, Tranströmer, Fried, Sorescu and so on, with one or two surprises. The translators are also known names such as Ted Hughes, Seamus Heaney or Scotland's own Edwin Morgan. But on the whole this is more of an opportunity missed than it should have been. Readers may well find something new and interesting to them here, and there are certainly no inferior poets presented, but it is less than the definitive volume which we seem to expect from Faber, more Alvarez's bedside book of European poetry in translation, focused on a Europe that has already passed into history. Where Dunn has clearly struggled to produce a sizeable tribute to Scottish poetry in the twentieth century, Alvarez seems to have settled for a more leisurely 'my top ten' approach.   *Robert Alan Jamieson*

Hard-Boiled Sweets

Rolling, Thomas Healy, Polygon, £7.95; *Swing Hammer Swing!*, Jeff Torrington, Secker & Warburg, £7.99; *Electric Brae — a Modern Romance*, Andrew Greig, Canongate Press, £14.95

Having read Healy's first novel, *It Might have been Jerusalem*, it was no surprise to find much of the same in *Rolling*. As before, the

action is characterised by a seemingly inevitable vileness and degradation both human and urban. This time around, however, the horror and squalor is not exclusively Glaswegian but takes on a continental flavour as the novel's grim Glaswegian protagonist's travels take him to Europe and beyond.

Vicious quaffing sessions and Hell's leftover hangovers populate most of the book's pages and central character Michael's waking hours with a monotonous inevitability that is enough to make the reader want to turn to drink. From early adolescence Michael flirts with alcohol, crime, schoolgirls, young boys and even has a brief affair with fatherhood until his embryonic child becomes another number on a list recording teenage abortions.

Not content with suffering from hangovers in Glasgow, Michael's raging thirst takes him abroad to sup in most of southern Europe, some of Australia and even as far afield as Asia. Of course on the way he tackles a few doses of "virulent clap", fathers a couple of children, writes a novel, has his life saved by a pair of lesbians and fornicates with numerous women apparently turned on by beery breath and absence of personal hygiene.

Eventually tiring of the "high life" abroad, Michael returns to the inviting greyness of Glasgow's slums and finds comfort in the taste of methylated spirits. And so we leave poor Michael with his shadow of a life wrecked by booze and a strong adherence to the ideal of the "Glasgow Hard Man". And yet it is difficult to feel sympathy for the man since there is little opportunity to look into the mind of Michael. We only get as far as being told that he "was a much nicer boy then than I was now as a man" (hardly bonding material) before he starts on another bender. As a history of hangovers *Rolling* is no doubt sufficient but as a study of long-term alcoholism, I'm afraid it is not.

Swing Hammer Swing! travels along very similar paths except that the drinking, gambling and fighting remains in the Gorbals. There has been much talk of this novel and even more about its author Jeff Torrington. From the Gorbals himself, Torrington made his first trip to London to accept prizes for this first novel and has been the focus of much media interest because of this.

Why this should be is puzzling. Many books have been written about the terrible conditions of working-class Glasgow and Glasgow itself is no stranger to literary talent. And *Swing Hammer Swing!* does not seem so very different to the likes of Healy's works mentioned above – it has no startling revelations to tell about life in the Gorbals. (Perhaps the London-minded find the idea of Gorbals man writing about a Gorbals they know little of as something novel and as ripe to hype and patronise as the taxi-driver who became champion of Mastermind some years back.)

Swing Hammer Swing! is all very macho and all very tough. Thomas Clay is the man who lives in the threatening underworld of a Gorbals threatened itself by demolition and by the drunken violence of its remaining inhabitants. Just like Healy's Michael, Torrington's Mr Clay has written a novel too. Uncanny that beneath all these Glasgow Hard Men there are rampant Dostoevskys just waiting to get out.

Whether this is coincidence or a shared vision into the nature of the urban rough and tough it is difficult to judge. Still, Torrington does write with a difference even if his subject seems familiar. His language fuses Glasgow patter with a dry and ironic blend of "moviespeak". This keeps the pace of the novel buoyant, which is helpful in a story with little plot but a series of alcohol-soaked events.

Torrington's sense of irony and humour are sharp and dry. Sarcastic comments and biting put-downs bring a wry smile to the lips but unfortunately do little to distract from the tedium of male toughness and arrogance that pervades throughout its vomit-strewn and unshaven pages.

Thankfully there's little trace of the Glasgow Hard Man in Andrew Greig's *Electric Brae – A Modern Romance*. As its title implies this is a novel about love – about the love between family, friends and lovers. Such bonds are explored through a handful of characters whose common link is a Scottish base either through birth or migration.

Set in the '80s, it traces the changing lives of its characters both emotionally and geographically from Shetland to the Borders. Jimmy is the narrator and central character at the heart of the book's emotional centre. Despite the appearance of another male chief

94

protagonist, *Electric Brae* is not male-centred like the novels of Healy and Torrington – whose only mention of women is detrimental or unavoidable since their male characters are having sex with them.

Jimmy's friendships with both men and women reveal an ultimate empathy with the human condition as he learns to cope with feelings of loss, desire, love and all their emotional sidekicks. Perhaps what is most significant in his coming to terms with all his emotions is his realisation of the constrictions that society lays upon men in their supposed limited emotional attributes.

Jimmy successfully manages to break this code in his relationships which ultimately makes this a hopeful novel. It is refreshing too, in its candid portrayal of friendships between men and its successful breaking down of the homophobic myth that love between men can exist only as homosexual love. Unashamedly tender at times, the book also confronts humanity's uglier emotions and in doing so proves itself to be enlightened, moving and worthy of several readings.

Sara Evans

The Long And Short Of It

A Friend of Humanity and other stories, George Friel, Polygon, £7.95; *Last Orders*, James Meek, Polygon, £7.95; *The Laughing Playmate*, ed ?, HarperCollins, £7.99; *The Penguin Book of Modern Women's Short Stories*, ed Susan Hill, Penguin, £5.99; *The Woman's Hour Book of short Stories 2*, ed Pat McLoughlin, BBC Books, £5.99

George Friel often had problems getting his short stories published. Polygon, playing an archival role, has published 21 of his stories from 'You can see it for yourself' (1935) through, more or less chronologically, to 'A couple of old bigots' (*Chapman*, 1976). In a useful introduction, Gordon Jarvie outlines the debt that these early stories owe to James Joyce. Friel kept a diary comparing his Glasgow stories of the 1930s with *Dubliners*, in terms of subject-matter, length and a listing of "subjects to be covered". That influence is clearest in a story like 'Home', about class dif-

ference and indifference with a similarity to Joyce's 'Clay', but Joyce's presence undercuts Jarvie's assertion that Friel tries to give us a picture of a world that is 'true' to working-class Glasgow. More often, like Joyce's, Friel's world is limpid, wan and sentimentalised.

At their best these stories can sacrifice the passive early-Joycean mode for a strong vein of unsettling humour. In a story like 'Unemployed' in which a young man kills his embittered, goading mother the story is turned away from its implicit social comment by a chorus of unsympathetic unemployed men, who, at the end of the story, hear the news and mock the boy. The stories that lack that edge sink uncontrollably into sub-Joycean pathos.

Livelier stories are set around the Plottel family who, with their spendthrift father and dominant mother, had much in common with Friel's own family. 'Mr Plottel's Benefit Concert' is a comedy telling how Plottel organises a concert with his show-business friends, hoping to pocket the proceeds. Seen through the eyes of his discomfited younger son, veering between cynicism and hope in his attitude to his father, family tension is well conveyed, as it is in 'Brothers', another Plottel tale.

This collection is worth reading for the stories in which Friel transcends the Joycean model, and also for the light which some of them shed upon the novels (say in the relationship between the protagonists of 'You can see it for yourself' and between Mr Alfred and Rose Weipers in *Mr Alfred MA*), Jarvie's assessment that had Friel lived longer or later, he would have found it easier for his stories to get a hearing along with Gray and Kelman needs to be taken with a large pinch of salt: Friel's style seems dated, his point of view is uncomfortably patronising and his stories lack energy. Today's Glasgow writers are ploughing a very different furrow.

In *Last Orders* James Meek, a journalist as well as a fiction writer, shows an admirable ability to turn empty phrases and ideas inside out. The situations in Meek's stories are absurdist and arbitrary. His protagonists tend to be the victims of mechanical and bizarre events. Often the disjointed worlds are so private that they can only be seen by the protagonist. In the title story, a man drinking in his local finds that the bar is shutting up and last orders being taken, but only for him: his friends drink on as he is pushed to the door.

Several titles (like 'The War Between Edinburgh and Glasgow') suggest a narrative about public events, when the stories are in fact essentially private. In 'Recruitment in Troubled Times' the bizarre world is the public one, and the protagonist is trying to behave normally in the midst of it. The story is set in an authoritarian Catholic Scottish state which oppresses and occupies its English neighbour and has to contend with a number of virulent English nationalist guerillas. The action revolves around an interview to appoint a new State Torturer, and focuses on the tension between the interviewer, his deputy, and the "applicant". The dystopian setting, and the comedy, are brilliantly achieved.

The best stories in *The Laughing Playmate*, the HarperCollins collection of Scottish Short Stories for 1992, tend to be Meekish rather than Frielish: slightly surreal, energetic and absurd rather than limpid and sensitive. 'I Eat My Peas With Honey' by Georgina McIntosh is a crackling story of a teenage girl's incarceration in a mental hospital after wrapping her brother's car around a tree. Her straining at the rules and regulations of the hospital is indicated by the text breaking out of prose and into limericks, songs and dramatic dialogues. 'The Fantasy Door' by Alison Armstrong is another impressive tale about being kept locked up, this time in a school for wayward girls, which turns into a hectic meditation on imagination, repression and reality. The protagonist, inside for setting fire to her father's girlfriend's boutique, fights against being turned into one of the "Gingerbread Girls", pacified and neutered by fear and the repressive environment of the school. Interestingly, the most successful stories here are the most formally innovative, though Iain Crichton Smith's story 'The German Hospital' is particularly well-measured, and more threatening than the more overt chillers. The collection is stylistically varied, geographically wide-ranging (from Nigeria to Rhodesia, Australia and Italy) but inevitably uneven and, despite its title, there are precious few laughs.

Susan Hill's selection, as editor of *The Penguin Book of Modern Women's Short Stories*, addresses a feeble range of social concerns.

The emphasis of Hill's introduction is profoundly suburban. She commends Fay Weldon's story 'Weekend' thus: "no one writes with greater trenchancy and insight of the North London middle classes", with no hint of tongue in cheek; her description of a thoroughly colourless A S Byatt story, 'The July Ghost', as "one of the finest ghost stories written this century" is preposterous.

On occasion, the stories with the narrowest range produce the best moments. Elizabeth Taylor's 'The Devastating Boys', about a meek professor's wife taking two black boys from London for a country holiday, is a gentle and generous comedy, while Claire Boylan's story, 'Some Retired Ladies on a Tour', is savagely witty and macabre. Muriel Spark is similarly barbed in 'The Black Madonna', and Jessie Kesson's lyric story, 'Stormy Weather', introduces a whole new mind-set. But these are exceptions. If you want a book of suburban English short stories, look no further than this.

The contents of the *Woman's Hour Book of Short Stories 2* have been through the selection process twice, once as prose pieces chosen to be read on radio and then, as the pick of the readings, assembled into a prose collection. The stories' formal constraints all stem from that previous life as a piece of speech. Each story is of a similar length. Stories with a straightforward narrative voice tend to prevail over more complex narrative styles. Some display a rather hackneyed twist-in-the-tale. The quality is high, the social settings more varied than in the Penguin collection, though the thematic arrangement reflects a certain ancient/modern schizophrenia as the thematic groups seem dated.

Highlights are Sylvia Townsend Warner's slight but intriguing 'A View of Exmoor', Nina Fitzpatrick's Irish family romance 'How Slattery Tricked his Mother into Touching Him' and Deborah Moggach's tale of frustrated family life 'Some Day my Prince Will Come'.

The collection is solid, readable and rather dull. A little tartness would have broken up the surface. The introduction makes much of the "warming", "touching" qualities of many of these stories, and too often this collection reproduces the conventions that can make the Woman's Hour story such a cloying listen.

David Stenhouse

SCOTLAND`S QUALITY THEATRE QUARTERLY

COMPLETE PLAYSCRIPT / LIVELY DEBATE / IN-DEPTH INTERVIEWS

BRIAN COX READS

theatre

S C O T L A N D

SO SHOULD YOU!

I wish to subscribe to *THEATRE SCOTLAND*, starting from the NEXT ISSUE /

CURRENT ISSUE* (delete as applicable) . I enclose a cheque payable to *THEATRE*

SCOTLAND for £ [   ]   £13 for four issues, (£20 overseas surface / £30 airmail)

NAME   . . . .

ADDRESS   . . . .

POSTCODE

. . . .

THEATRE SCOTLAND, 9a ANNANDALE STREET, EDINBURGH EH7 4AW (BOX CH)

Theatre Roundup

If 1992 was a year of transition in Scottish theatre, then the autumn season provided an early hint of what could be in store for the year to come. Whether it was Mull Little Theatre, the Brunton, Scottish Youth Theatre, Dundee Rep, 7:84, Grey Coast Theatre, TAG, Winged Horse or the Edinburgh International Festival, new artistic directors had begun to make their presence felt in established organisations by the end of the year. Once Kenny Ireland takes the reins at Edinburgh's Royal Lyceum at the end of April, the transition will perhaps be complete. Whatever happens, it's reasonable to expect a greater degree of confidence and adventurousness as the various appointees build on their successes.

The man who landed the hardest job in Scottish theatre was Hamish Glen, who inherited the crisis-ridden Dundee Rep and set about attracting back a disillusioned audience. It may be premature to say, but in his first brief season of office, Glen seems to have revitalised a theatre whose audience figures had sunk to perilous levels before he took over at the end of the summer. Bringing with him a policy that characterised his work with Winged Horse – a commitment to European and American classics performed in a punchy, accessible and usually Scottish-accented style; and support for modern, home-grown playwrights – Glen has strengthened the theatre's traditional commitment to community work, not least in the appointment of Michael Duke as Assistant Director whose remit is to 'direct all community activities and liaise with the community dance team'.

The policy seems to be paying off and Glen is already ahead of himself in his plan to get audiences back into the theatre before he feels confident enough to broaden the range of work he programmes. His debut production of CP Taylor's *Walter* might have missed the mark when it opened in the Edinburgh Festival, but by the time it transferred to Dundee it had acquired a focus and pace that set him off to a confident start. The promise of his turbulent and uncompromising *Who's Afraid of Virginia Woolf?*, performed with Scots accents, was confirmed with a glorious revival of *Tartuffe*, exciting and fast-paced in vibrant

bravura Scots, in a version first commissioned by the Royal Lyceum in 1985 from Liz Lochhead (who herself enjoyed a healthy season with revivals of *Mary Queen of Scots Got Her head Chopped Off* at Perth and *The Big Picture* at the Brunton). And the new year has begun as the Rep means to go on, with a highly-rated staging of *Hard Times* directed by Communicado's Gerry Mulgrew.

Taking up Scotland's small-scale theatre gap left by the Traverse's move to their new premises, The Citizens' Theatre continues its policy of presenting three plays at a time, making use of the two additional studio spaces it opened this time last year. The risky, experimental nature of the work has led to inconsistent attendance rates and there is a worry that the existing audience has been divided rather that a new crowd attracted. Undoubtedly one of the most successful productions was the dramatisation of Iain Banks' Gothic novel *The Wasp Factory* which was a box office sell-out with a young, cultish audience, and has now been revived for a second run in the spring season. Disturbing and casually brutal, Malcolm Sutherland's production left the critical fraternity rather cold, but appealed to its more worldly-wise audience. The revival of Pinter's *The Birthday Party*, thirty years after it was first produced, was a revelation in a production by designer Antony McDonald who brought it to life with *Twin Peaks* topicality. In the close intimacy of the Circle Studio, Pinter's play of black humour and menace was given a particularly contemporary chill with the sinister softly-spoken Irish of McCann (Henry Ian Cusick), who, with the schizophrenic Goldberg (Andrew Joseph), created an atmosphere of absurdity and terror, reinforced by the claustrophobia and intensity of the direction.

With productions ranging from tried and tested standards (Shaw's *Major Barbara*) to the established but still radical (Beckett's *Happy Days*), from the bizarre and experimental (*The Home Show Pieces*) to the faithful treatment of modern classics (*Not About Heroes*), the Citz has reinvented itself and kept its edge as the one place in Scotland where even the failures are *interesting* failures.

Edinburgh's Royal Lyceum also gave us a Pinter revival. *Old Times* explored the struggle for power and dominance in intimate relationships between husband, wife, and mutual friend, in that shifting pattern of two against one which informs many of Pinter's plays. Hugh Hodgart directed a subtle and sensitive production which drew attention to the cloying desperation of stagnant relationships, while doing much justice to Pinter's surreal sense of humour. Neil Bartlett's adaptation of Moliere's *School For Wives*, directed by Ian Wooldridge, attempted to hit a note of cartoon burlesque, but for all its local references and in-jokes, it was laboured and relentless. The revival of *Laurel and Hardy*, Tom McGrath's faithful and affectionate tribute to the great comic clowns, didn't match the sublime brilliance of the originals, but probably won them some new fans nonetheless.

Robin Peoples is one of those directors trying to make his mark in a new theatre, having inherited the severely limited budget and out-of-town audience of Musselburgh's Brunton Theatre from the maverick Charles Nowosielski . The ex-SYT director played safe for his first season, but came up with a programme that was far from bland. One recalls his award-winning *Blood-Knot* in the Edinburgh Festival, while Pam Gems' *Piaf* and the Stoppard double-bill, *After Magritte* and *The Real Inspector Hound*, were interesting choices, if only mixed successes; and it is good to see a commitment to new writing so early on in Lara Jane Bunting's lyrical tribute to the life of Jean Armour in *Love But Her*, which began the spring season of plays by women writers.

The House Among the Stars at the Traverse confirms Michel Tremblay as one of the finest contemporary playwrights, his work particularly suited to a Scottish context and interpretation; and just the latest in a highly successful series of his plays given the Scots treatment by Bill Findlay and Martin Bowman, beginning with the Tron's international hit, *The Guid Sisters*, and continuing with *The Real Wurld* and *Hosanna*. Ian Brown's production, complimented by an outstanding set by Gerry Pilgrim that sustained the chronological shifts in this powerful and evocative play about the struggles toward sexual identity in and between generations of the same family, was a highlight of autumn at the Traverse.

Canada was the source of the Traverse's other big autumn hit, Brad Fraser's *Unidentified Human Remains and the True Nature of Love*. Set in Alberta, a town whose claim to fame is that it is home to the world's largest shopping mall, the play is a darkly erotic comic thriller about young people making sense of their lives and relationships. Perhaps not as profound or as radical as it purported to be, it nonetheless struck a chord with audiences, some of whom were caught snogging – empathetically no doubt – during the performance!

TAG's *Clockwork Orange* revived chilling memories of Burgess's novel and Kubrick's uncompromising film. Tony Graham's direction typically made dance an integral part of the performance – indeed this aspect was rather more successful than the verbal side – and, by the critics at least, it was deemed to make a more happy transition to the stage than *The Wasp Factory* that ran at the Citizens' simultaneously. TAG's multi-media work was consolidated in November when eighteen performers of all disciplines went through a three-week rehearsal project using Alasdair Gray's *Lanark* as source material. There was no performance, but the actors and dancers, and ultimately Scottish theatre, benefited greatly from the opportunity to learn, experiment and explore.

Meanwhile, those still in the world of conventional training have been showing promise in recent student productions at RSAMD and Queen Margaret College, and it is pleasing to see recent graduates making their debuts. A special mention must also be made of the excellent work of the Edinburgh student theatre Bedlam, and its link with the European Association of Students of Theatre. As Scotland seeks to develop its links with Europe, today's theatre students are outward-looking and outward-going: for example, Toby Gough, an outstandingly promising young director and producer, has recently returned from Moscow with his original and highly inventive award-winning *Grimm*, which was also revived at the Traverse. For all the production suffered from lack of tight editing, it was blessed with an energy and sense of living theatre from which many established professionals would do well to learn.

Mark Fisher (with Michael Ridings)

Pamphleteer

Published in the wake and the style of Alasdair Gray's *Why Scots Should Rule Scotland*, Paul H Scott's *Scotland in Europe – Dialogue with a Sceptical Friend* (Canongate, £4.95) is as patiently explanatory as its title suggests. Constructed in an interview-style debate with SF asking very leading questions to PHS, Paul takes us by the hand and guides us through areas of confusion and general party-political fudge like 'Why Independence?', 'Scotland too Small?' and 'The European Dimension'. This is an idiot's guide to independence (with the Europe angle thrown in) so I personally found it quite useful though most Independence-aware people would doubtless think it rather basic. Also added for good measure are sections on 'Independence – Why Not?' and 'Devolution – a Useful First Step?' which seems a rather obvious ruse to undermine any official points of view that deviate from the Nationalist position. PHS obviously knows what he's talking about as he produces many facts and figures to back himself up, and despite the technical stuff it slips down as easily as a Loch Fyne oyster. The conclusion is that any arguments opposing Scottish Independence are red herrings and that if only we had the chance we could transform Scotland into a prosperous nirvana of oil and fish. One chapter however seems to have slithered through his net – 'Equal Representation for Women in a Scottish Parliament – Why Not?'

Tom Nairn has also seen fit to publish a collection of his Monday articles from the *Scotsman* (Common Cause, £2.95). Called *Auld Enemies,* it is part of a series of pamphlets produced by common Cause which aim to make "Declarations" on "citizenship and democracy in Europe". Nairn's outspoken views on Independence will be known to many but the collection lends him a particularly powerful voice, brimming over with indignant vitriol.

Another crusading publication is Jeff Fallows' *Revolting Scotland* (Luath Press, £5.95), a cartoon history of the country and socio-political commentary *née* blatantly didactic and emotive propaganda. However I have no doubt that this book will effectively fulfil its author's motives. This is largely due to the quality of the drawing, which must surely be inspired by Japanese cartoonist Keiji Nakazawa whose *Barefoot Gen* books powerfully encapsulated the scale of horror created by the atom-bombing of Hiroshima. Next to Hergé, Nakazawa is often said to be one of the world's greatest cartoonists, so Fallow has chosen an admirable rôle-model. It's refreshing to see a strong new medium like this, even if it is just being used to tell the same old story.

Taranis Poetry have come out with two collections recently: *The Mating of Dinosaurs* (£5.99) by William Oliphant and Brian Whittingham's *Ergonomic Work Stations and Spinning Tea Cans* (£4.99).

Oliphant's collection includes some quite moving and poignant pieces. He is most accomplished when discussing old age, taking stock, and poetry itself. My favourite was the title poem which displays a consciousness of time passing, of history, and of his place in it. He adds soul and tenderness to the relentless wheel of evolution and the inevitability of extinction. A worrying aspect of his work is how often he takes a woman's voice, and though he does this with some compassion in 'Miscarriage' and 'Hysterectomy', I am wary of male authors' motives when they do not write about a woman's experience from their own point of view. Perhaps it is easier to express emotions through someone else's experience, or perhaps the poet merely assumes the right to talk for the woman?

Brian Whittingham charts his own progress through an industrial to a clerical career. He details his experience as – and observations of – the underdog in terse, manic verse. He also makes rather obvious and unnecessary use of concrete poetry to shove a point or two home. Tom Leonard fans will like this stuff as will nostalgics on reading 'Empties'. Rather too much beer, balls, and macaroon bars for my taste, though.

Four male poets and himself have been published by John Mingay at Raunchland Publications. *3x4* is a wee "magazine that gives you poetry without the padding". It includes some not-bad stuff if overall the material is a bit bleak, lonesome and self-indulgent. There seems to be some Irish comment and religious implication here, and the odd line of misogynist imagery. The best poems are Howard Wright's 'Scarecrow' and

Rupert Loydell's 'French Journal Excerpts'. John Mingay's own work, 'The Shadow No Longer Hurts', is an illustrated sequence-poem – a mixed-media presentation on a pile of thick tomato-red paper on which black abstract words alternate with bold abstract images. I *think* this is all making a bleak existentialist statement, but here's the first page:

Even the living moment
serenades catastrophe
in defiance of the night:

If I found that last poem inaccessible/incomprehensible, then David Kinloch's *Dustie Fute* (Vennel Press, £4.99) is pure gobbledygook. "In this sequence of poems a pot of yoghurt vanishes from a Paris windowsill and turns into an old Scots word for a fairground juggler." I can assure you this is as clear as it gets. These are contrived, reader-exclusive, deliberately obtuse (or maybe just drug-induced) babblings. My advice to David is to get some chlorpromazine down him. And here's why:

A freen is whileons widder-gleam,
whilesome watter.
Lat gang thi dounmaist souch
o August; a body
isna ae thi ben o an auch,
nakid licht, o burd-
bouky birks,
summer-cloks i thi snood; ...

Thank God for Rebel Inc Publications. Just when I was beginning to feel overwhelmed by self-indulgent, hard-done-by, self-pitying crap, I opened Barry Graham's *Pigeon* (£1) and started to smirk. This is an eight-page epic pigeon's-eye view of the state of Scotland, a pigeon who

... has the Buddha-nature.
He rarely rages against what he can't change,
though it saddens him and makes him tired.

This pigeon takes a flight over Edinburgh and delivers an all-encompassing critique of our social ills with anarchy and sarcasm, commenting even on the literary scene:

where this poem will be sneered at as
didactic and unsubtle by scumbag illiterati
who wouldn't recognise a major poem if it
walked up to them in broad daylight
and shagged them up the arse.

Rebel Inc's second offering, *Burn it Down*, comes from Kevin Williamson, who writes with a refreshingly contemptuous pen about Ravenscraig, dole queues and sexist comedians: "When Benny Hill died I had a right good laugh". He captures more tragic and ludicrous truth in his few hilarious words than a century of serious, worthy Scottish writers. Recommended are 'Sweet Rebel Music' and 'Go on yersels and burn the whole fucking country to the ground' (about the LA riots). Incidentally Rebel Inc have, to their credit, picked up on Alison Kermack who is certain to be one of the next really big Scottish writers.

Next, and in direct contrast to the previous gutsy humour, comes *Hoots Mon!*, a collection of so-called humorous Scottish poems (ed Colin McLeod). These poems combine an elementary sense of rhythm and rhyme with a primary-school sense of humour. This uniformly twee selection might make an ideal birthday gift for Great Auntie Moira, you can probably find it beside the haggis in any Loch Ness gift shop.

Finally to some really good poetry. Hidden beneath the pile of mediocre, macho, nationalist publications is *Pomegranate* (Stramullion, £4.95 and worth every penny) – "poems by Pomegranate Women's Writing Group". Defying the usual (and unjustified) criticism that poetry of women's experience is merely therapeutic and subjective, this collection has to be one of the most powerful, intelligent, astute, spiritual, moving, angry, funny and IMPORTANT anthologies Scotland has produced in recent years. It is telling that the only Scottish women's poetry in this *Pamphleteer* is in an anthology; and the sad fact is that Stramullion now only exists to publish occasionally. The lack of published new Scottish women writers and the lack of a Scottish women's press are not unrelated factors.

Ranting aside, I'd recommend Rebecca Wilson's 'Turning Point', Jo Sumners 'On Being Hollow', Ruth McIlroy's 'Annunciation', Maggie Christie's 'Stone Circle', Margaret Elphinstone's 'Lilies' and Paula Jennings 'Assertively Trained', from which these lines:

... they will know us by our squawks and brashly
gleaming beaks
as we dive
impolitely accurate
at the muscled heart of power.

Charlotte Ross

Catalogue

Plainly the Queen was not crowned on the *real* Stone of Scone – why else would things be as they are now? We trust that Canongate have respectfully forwarded a copy of *The Search for the Stone of Destiny* (Pat Gerber, with photos by Andrew Morris, £13.95) to Balmoral to aid those courtiers not too busy leaking stories to the press to get out and look for the real one.

The *Chambers Book of Facts* (Chambers, £11.99) doesn't say anything about the real stone being at Westminster. All sorts of things that you couldn't possibly know that you wanted to know are shoehorned into its not-so-slim covers covering 280 fields of interest (or indifference as the case may be). On fact-facts it's fine: many interesting things including a list of recent environmental disasters which implies that wherever there is nuclear power, there is nuclear disaster. Having been told all those years ago that ane of these were likely per thousand years, the human race can surely look forward to countless thousands of disaster-free years from now on. Not.

When it comes to summarising the world's philosophers' lives in one sentence –

Diogenes (412–323BC) Greek, born Sinope, Pontus. Continued the pre-Socratic tradition of speculation about the primary constituent of the world, which he identified as air, operating as an active and intelligent life-force.

you wonder whether this is the first place you'd look that kind of thing up. Some of the scientific information is a bit sketchy too: okay, so a Parsec is approximately 3.26 light years, but *why*?

This reminds me of *James Burke's Connections* for some reason – six BBC programmes of embarrassingly tendentious links from one item to another, showing how the humble shoe-horn connects with *Voyager II*'s mission to Jupiter (apocryphal example). Which leads me conveniently to the *International Women's Art Diary 1993* (Open Letters, £7.99). If you are as disorganised as I am, it's not too late to get a copy, full of stunning image, and space to write things. (What did you expect?)

Speaking of striking images, compare the photograph of Robert Louis Stevenson on the cover of Ian Bell's biography *Dreams of Exile* (Mainstream, £14.99) and the author's own on the inside back. Notwithstanding the blurb-writer's use of the word 'attempt' twice in one paragraph on the jacket, and a conventionally journalistic narrative style, Bell draws on a wide range of sources and succeeds in conveying a rounded portrait of the man – he is, after all, a *good* journalist. *The Master of Ballantrae* has just appeared as a Canongate Classic, by the way (£4.95).

God knows what kind of a nit views Mozart as either 'divine idiot' or 'journeyman tune-smith' (the blurb-writer strikes again), but let them read Nicholas Till's admirable *Mozart and the Enlightenment* (Faber, £30), which places Mozart's operas in their cultural/political/intellectual/sociological context rather as John Purser achieves in *Scotland's Music*. It's a revealing picture of the pressures and influences no great creator can ignore.

Let me list some of the names you'll find in Michael Hamburger's autobiography *String of Beginnings* (Skoob, £10.99), a reprint of Carcanet's 1973 original: Francis Bacon, Robert Graves, WS Graham, George Barker, Dylan Thomas. Aside from the more obvious bohemian connection, the company implies (correctly) that this is a diverting read on various levels. His translations of Günter Eich, meantime, are published in *Pigeons and Moles* by Skoob (£7.99), a collection including prose, poetry and playwriting.

Some Recent Attacks (AK Press, £4.50) is a collection of essays by James Kelman, chewing at a range of bone-headed conceits, veering in tone from the hound of Hell through, frankly, to Spike (as in Tom & Jerry) occasionally. Mostly, though, these are tough, effective and just attacks, such as 'English Literature and the Small Coterie' with its reflections on the Salman Rushdie *fatwah*.

Richard Poirier's *Poetry and Pragmatism* (Faber, £20) just happens to be next in the pile. Collated from his TS Eliot lectures at Kent University and Gauss Seminars at Princeton, The bone Poirier sucks thoughtfully upon is a line of linguistic philosophy drawn through Emerson, William James, Gertude Stein and the criticism of Kenneth Burke, which he calls linguistic scepticism. Poirer's own language is delightful: the warm side of dusty, and terse.

Seeing Les Murray (*Collected Poems*, Carcanet, £18.95) was born in New South Wales,

GAIRM PUBLICATIONS

Clann a' Phroifeasair (The Professor's Children)

Suitable for ages 10-14, describes the assorted escapades of Hugh and Anna on the island of Oronsay, along with their personal flying machines. (The sequel, *Talfasg*, follows their adventures in Time). An Irish language edition has just been published in Connemara, and is also available through GAIRM.

Spuirean na h-Iolaire (Claws of the Eagle)

A murder and mystery thriller, involving a network of fascist plotters throughout the country.

"(The) underlying sense of moral seriousness gives Iain MacLeòid's story its power."

Meg Bateman, *CHAPMAN*

Coinneach Odhar

An imaginative recreation of the life and times of the Brahan Seer.

"a valuable quarry for the anthropological investigation this entire prophetic tradition calls for. It hardly needs to be added that the stories themselves have an intrinsic interest as fiction."

John MacInnes, *Books in Scotland*

A' Mheanbhchuileag

A long philosophical poem by Fearghas MacFhionnlaigh, with religious and nationalist themes.

"... undoubtedly one of the major Gaelic poems this century".

Ronald Black, *The History of Scottish Literature Vol 4*

Bardachd na Roinn Eòrpa An Gàidhlig

Poems from over twenty European languages, representing fifty-five poets, ranging from Ancient Greece to modern times. Includes Sappho, Brecht, Dafydd ap Gwilym, Hölderlin, Rilke, Garcia Lorca, MacDiarmid, Montale, Neruda, Shakespeare, Pásternak, Yeats and many, many more.

"This anthology is proof of the continuing vitality of Gaelic literature."

John MacInnes, *The Scotsman*

Appendix to Dwelly (1991)

The previously unpublished supplement to Dwelly's Illustrated Dictionary, by far the most comprehensive available. The Appendix offers the same richness of material, including all sorts of ritual names and expressions. There is an amusing account of the remorseless hospitality formerly endured by house-guests in the Highlands before breakfasting – "... on waking, gave him the *gloc-nide* (nest-gulp), and after he gave the *deoch air uilinn* (drink on elbow), the guest would rise up in bed. Before putting on his clothes, he got the *deoch chas-ruisgte* (barefoot drink), and then before taking breakfast it was the duty of all to take another dram, the *clach-bhleith* (sharpening, or whet-stone)." Presumaby the custom pre-dated modern excise duties!

"... a joy to possess"   Aonghas MacNeacail, *The Herald*

"... A real treasure-trove"   J. MacInnes, *Books in Scotland*

GAIRM PUBLICATIONS
29 WATERLOO ST.
GLASGOW
G2 6BZ
Telephone or Fax (041) 221-1971

and a poem called 'Vindaloo in Merthyr Tyd-fil' I sensed another James Burke, and found myself in a disconcertingly familiar world, created to perfection: "...I spooned the chicken of Hell/in a sauce of rich yellow brim-stone..." ... reminded me of a Fhal (the order that makes waiters laugh) I once endured in Swindon in Welsh company... Murray's writ-ing is pithy, vigorous, humane; his scope wide-ranging. To Siberia: chill winds blow through *The Collected Poems 1952–1990* (Mainstream, £18) of Yevgeny Yevtuschenko, though this massively impressive volume, featuring translations by several internation-ally distinguished poets, still isn't a substitute for the beautiful sound of the original Russian.

David Lindsay's *A Voyage to Arcturus*, another of that breed, the underrated Scottish novel, is available again (Canongate Classics, £4.95). In the guise of science fiction Lindsay explores human emotions, not least disgust, as his hero Maskull challenges "baseness mas-querading as nature... the Devil masquerading as God", as J B Pick's introduction has it. From Secker & Warburg, the urbane prose of Saul Bellow in *Something to Remember Me By* (£13.99). Bellow's brief foreword expounds on the virtues of, well, brevity in a world he describes containing *inter alia* "giant news-stands... virtually thatched with magazines."

A Scottish clock strikes a chime as Kent Thompson, introducing *Engaged Elsewhere* (Quarry Press, Ontario, £?) describes the dif-ficulty of defining Canadian literature without reference to the large neighbour underneath. The book contains short stories by Canadians abroad. Below the harmless surface of the col-lection's thesis – that Canadians are remarka-bly good at living in and writing about foreign countries — are a few piranhas waiting to munch on carelessly-strewn assumptions, such as 'Living in New York means you are no longer Canadian'.

Unusually, for a Canongate Classic, *Three Scottish Poets – MacCaig, Morgan, Lochhead* (£4.95) is not a reprint as such, but a selection from their work with notes and brief introduc-tions by Roderick Watson. Although not unwelcome, the book's *raison d'être* seems a little vague. Serge Baudot's bilingual anthol-ogy *Six Poetes Ecossais*, harbouring MacCaig again, Crichton Smith, Mackay Brown, Conn,

Dunn et Butlin, is plainer in its mission to make Scottish poetry available to the French-speaking world. Anything but poetic, its value marred by inadequate bibliographical infor-mation, is Charlotte Reid's *List of Plays in Scots* compiled for the Scots Language Soci-ety and shoddily published by Glasgow City Libraries. It's in three sections, covering Plays written in Scots since 1900, plays translated into Scots, and Plays in Scots held in manu-script at libraries. This does Scots and the SLS few favours. In similar klepto vein, though no criticism should be imputed from its proxim-ity to the above, from Merchiston Publishing *Imprints in Time – a History of Scottish Pub-lishers Past and Present* (£6.95) has been col-lated by BA Publishing students at Napier Poly, focussing on people rather than houses, and ranging from the 16th century to the likes of Callum Macdonald, Stephanie Wolfe-Mur-ray and Bill Campbell.

The back cover of W J West's *The Larger Evils – 1984: the truth behind the satire* reads like the kind of thing you find on Holy-Blood-Holy-Grail-hysterical-historical-conspiracy-theory-type literature. That's just what's inside. Not a credit to Canongate, moved to publish it (£14.95), at a guess, on account of Orwell spending some time on Jura once. Mick McCluskey's *The Scheme-Hopper's Survival Guide* is not big enough to use as an offensive weapon, so the wisdom contained inside may prove essential. It's actually great fun, making extensive use of the Dundee vernacular, and copiously illustrated by Belinda Langlands: a kind of comic-book ethnography running through Dundee's schemes one by one giving tips on food, drink, buses, tribes etc.

Hello *The Virago Book of Wicked Verse* (£?) edited by Jill Dawson – warmly recom-mended; and don't jump to the conclusion that it's all about sex: meditate upon the title. From across the centuries and continents it gathers such writers as Sappho, Aphra Behn, Dorothy Parker, Eunice de Souza, Jackie Kay... pity about the solemn introduction. *Enfin*, from Pavilion (£9.99) comes *Bittersweet Within My Heart*, the collected poems of Mary, Queen of Scots, translated and edited by Robin Bell: Goddammit, does a woman have to be a queen before she can get her poetry published, and posthumously at that?

Notes on Contributors

Roy Allen: After spending 15 years in the oil industry, being nearly 40, he has "opted out" to a remote farmhouse where, whilst working on his second novel, he is desperately seeking an agent for the first.

Gavin Bowd: Teaches and writes in Paris after Galashiels, St Andrews and ten years of Communism.

Janet Caird: Scottish poet, novelist and writer of children's fiction; died 1992.

Vuyelwa Carlin: Born in 1949, grew up in Uganda. Works in Shrophire boarding school, first collection *Midas' Daughter*, Seren 1991.

Peter Cudmore: Composer & writer; affable, kind to cats.

John Dixon: His recent collection of poems, *Scots Baronial,* is published by Polygon.

Antonia Dodds: born 1969 in Edinburgh and educated there. She is currently a volunteer in mental health after studying English.

Alastair Dunnett: Journalist, author and playwright. One-time editor of both the *Daily Record* and *The Scotsman.*

Sara Evans: Freelance writer, editorial assistant at *Cencrastus.*

Mark Fisher is Managing Editor of *Theatre Scotland* and a contributor to *The List.*

Rab Fulton: Works as a male model in Glasgow – contact *Chapman* for details.

William Imray: Church organist, previously lecturer. Poems published in Scots, English, Gaidhlig and Latin.

Robert Alan Jamieson: Two legs, two arms... poet, novelist, translator: lives in South Queensferry, originally from Shetland.

Robin Jenkins: Born 1912, taught in Afghanistan, Spain and North Borneo. Latest novel *Willie Hogg* to be published by Polygon in October.

Patrica Mudge: Freelance writer, resident of San Francisco, writing a biography of the Muirs.

Mairi NicGumaraid: Born 1955 in Lewis. Poetry widely published in Scotland and Ireland. Her first adult novel *Clann Iseabail* is to be published by Acair.

Stuart A Paterson: Born 1966 Truro, raised Ayrshire. Co-edits the new literary magazine *Spectrum.* Won a Gregory Award in 1992 – has been drunk and incapable ever since.

William J Rae: Writer of many fables in Scots. Twenty so far, others pending...

Michael Ridings is a tutor in English at both Edinburgh and the Open Universities.

Charlotte Ross: co-editor, Harpies & Quines and part-time fish waitress.

Maggie Stephen: 24, lives and sometimes works in St Andrews, Fife. Occupations range from toothbrush inspector to yoga instructor – both enlightening in their own way.

Elspeth Stewart: Now writing full-time – currently up to one-and-a-half unpublished novels. Works in a lochside hut in Galloway; previously often distracted from writing by teaching.

George Smith: Born Dundee, 1958. Football fan, part-time poet, frustrated musician, ex-sailor, and lifer in HMP Edinburgh.

Catriona Soukup: attended Edinburgh University during the war; now lives in France.

Lumir Soukup: Secretary to Jan Masaryk before leaving Czechoslovakia in 1938; senior lecturer in Czech at Glasgow University for many years; died 1991.

David Stenhouse: engaged on PhD at Edinburgh University, having previously worked at BBC Edinburgh – frequently brightens *Queen Street Garden* with his countenance.